Skills Practice
Workbook

**Level 4
Book 1**

McGraw Hill **SRA**

Columbus, OH

SRAonline.com

Send all inquiries to this address:
SRA/McGraw-Hill
4400 Easton Commons
Columbus, OH 43219-6188

ISBN: 978-0-07-610480-2
MHID: 0-07-610480-X

13 QLM 14

Table of Contents

Unit 1 Risks and Consequences

Unit 2 Nature's Delicate Balance

③ Unit 3 **A Changing America**

Name _____ Date _____

Suffixes *-ly* and *-ness*

Focus

- A **suffix** is an addition to the end of a word. (call*ing*)
- A **root word** is a word to which a suffix can be added. (*call*ing)
- Adding the suffix *-ly* to the end of words creates adverbs, which describe the way something occurs. (swift*ly*, expert*ly*)
- If the word ends in *y*, the *y* is changed to *i* before adding *-ly*. (*lucky, luckily*)
- If the word ends in *ic*, the letters *al* must be added after the *ic* and before the *-ly*. (*realistic, realistically*)
- The suffix *-ness* means "state of." Adding *-ness* to the word *happy* makes the word *happiness*, or the state of being happy.
- If the word ends in *y*, the *y* is changed to *i* before adding *-ness*. (*silly, silliness*)

Practice   **Remove the suffixes *-ly* and *-ness* from the following words, and write the words correctly on the lines provided.**

1. partially _____

2. sadness _____

3. craziness _____

4. attractiveness _____

5. speedily _____

6. graphically _____

7. greedily _____

8. bulkiness _____

Skills Practice 1 • Word Structure

Apply | **Complete each sentence with the correct form of each word.**

9. Carter (cautious, cautiously) _____ opened the back door and peered outside.

10. Do you have any (scientific, scientifically) _____ evidence to back up your theory?

11. Your (happy, happiness) _____ is very important to me.

12. I really wish she could give directions without being so (bossy, bossiness)

_____.

13. The two girls (blissful, blissfully) _____ lounged in the summer sun.

Add the suffix -ly or -ness to each root word. Then write each new word in a sentence.

14. angry _____

_____

15. artistic _____

_____

_____

16. noisy _____

_____

17. clear _____

_____

_____

Name _____ Date _____

Selection Vocabulary

Focus

pursued (pûr · sōōd') *v.* chased (page 27)

tides (tīdz) *n.* rise and fall of the sea (page 29)

lacking (la' · king) *v.* being without (page 32)

fiber (fī' · bûr) *n.* piece of cloth (page 32)

cover (ku' · vûr) *v.* to travel over (page 33)

deserted (di' · zûr · təd) *v.* having no people (page 34)

idly (īd · lē) *adv.* not doing anything (page 34)

dozed (dōzd) *v.* slept lightly (page 37)

Practice Circle the word in parentheses that best fits each sentence.

1. The lazy dog slept (lacking / idly) on the couch.

2. The bank robber was being (dozed / pursued) by the police officer.

3. All was quiet on the (deserted / idly) ship.

4. My family will (fiber / cover) more than one thousand miles on our trip this summer.

5. When the weather turned cold, Sarah used the (fiber / tides) as a blanket.

6. The cat yawned and (pursued / dozed) in the afternoon sun.

7. I would run the race, but I am (lacking / cover) good running shoes.

8. The (deserted / tides) are strong on the shore of this island.

Apply

Match each word on the left to its definition on the right.

1. fiber	a. being without
2. tides	b. chased
3. lacking	c. rise and fall of the sea
4. idly	d. to travel over
5. pursued	e. not doing anything
6. cover	f. slept lightly
7. deserted	g. piece of cloth
8. dozed	h. having no people

Write a sentence using at least one of the vocabulary words from this lesson.

_____

_____

Name _____ Date _____

Author's Point of View

Focus

Writers must decide the point of view from which a story is told. All stories are told through a narrator—the person who tells the story. The narrator can tell the story from

- the **third-person point of view.** The narrator is an outside observer and uses pronouns such as *he, she,* and *they* when telling the story.

- the **first-person point of view.** The narrator is a character in the story and uses pronouns such as *I, me,* and *my* when telling the story.

Practice A

Look through "Island of the Blue Dolphins." Find three sentences that show the author's point of view. Write the page number, the sentence, and the point of view in the spaces below.

1. Page: _____ Point of view: _____

Sentence: _____

_____

2. Page: _____ Point of view: _____

Sentence: _____

_____

3. Page: _____ Point of view: _____

Sentence: _____

_____

Practice B

Read the following passage. Answer the questions about the author's point of view.

My mom and I planted a flower garden in the vacant lot at the end of the block. We knew it was a risky project because dogs or pranksters might dig up the flowers. But to my mom and me, the risk was worth taking. The colorful flowers added beauty to our neighborhood.

4. What is the author's point of view? _____

5. What words tell you the author's point of view?

_____

Apply

Rewrite the above passage using the third-person point of view.

_____

_____

_____

_____

_____

_____

_____

_____

_____

_____

_____

Name _____ Date _____

Generating Questions to Investigate

What other questions about risks and consequences would you like to learn more about? Write them here.

_____

_____

_____

_____

Now think about these questions. Are there people whom you admire because they take risks? Who are they? What risks have they taken?

Person	Risk
_____	_____
_____	_____

Below are more questions to think about:

- Does everyone agree on what a risk is?
- Do you have to be a certain kind of person to take risks?
- Can you do things to make a risk less risky?

Think of ways in which you could find anwers to these questions. Write them here.

_____

_____

Choosing Appropriate Sources

Make a list of topics that you want to learn more about from "Island of the Blue Dolphins." Some possible topics to investigate include the author of the story or the ways dolphins communicate.

Think of topics you would like to learn more about. Write three topics here.

_____

_____

Choose the topic you would most like to learn about.

_____

There are many sources you can use to investigate your favorite topic.

Encyclopedia	Newspapers	Interviews
Book	Dictionary	DVDs and videotapes
Magazines	Internet	Pamphlets and brochures

Choose two sources you could use to investigate your topic.

_____

What type of information do these sources contain?

_____

_____

What might you learn from these sources about your topic?

_____

_____

Name _____ Date _____

Writing Realistic Fiction

Think **Audience: Who** will read your realistic fiction?

_____

Purpose: What is your reason for writing a realistic fiction story?

_____

Prewriting Use this graphic organizer to organize the traits of your main character. Write the character's name in the circle. Then, write the character's traits on the branches.

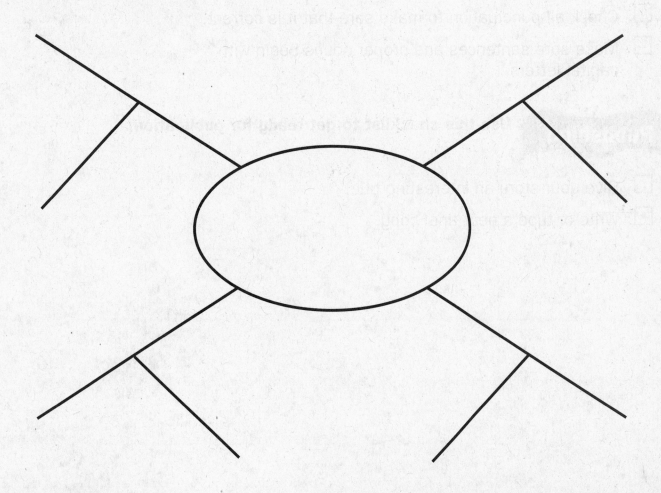

Revising

Use this checklist to revise your story.

- ☐ Do your characters seem like real people?
- ☐ Do your characters have clear motives?
- ☐ Do you use precise nouns, verbs, adjectives, and adverbs to bring the characters to life?
- ☐ Is your opening paragraph clear, and does it grab the reader's attention?

Editing/Proofreading

Use this checklist to correct mistakes. Use proofreader's marks as you read your first draft.

- ☐ Make sure that all words are spelled correctly.
- ☐ Check all punctuation to make sure that it is correct.
- ☐ Make sure sentences and proper nouns begin with capital letters.

Publishing

Use this checklist to get ready for publication.

- ☐ Give your story an interesting title.
- ☐ Write or type a neat final copy.

Name _____ Date _____

Spelling

Focus

- Remember the suffixes *-ous* and *–ful* mean *full of*
- Remember the suffix *-ly* means *in a certain way*
- Remember the suffix *–ment* means *the result of an action*
- Remember the suffix *–less* means *without*

The suffixes *–ous, -ful, -ly, -ment* and *–less* can be added to a root word without changing the spelling of that root word. Adding a suffix to a root word will change the word's meaning.

Practice A Sort the spelling words under each suffix.

-ous

1. _____
2. _____
3. _____
4. _____

-ful

5. _____
6. _____
7. _____
8. _____

-ly

9. _____
10. _____
11. _____
12. _____

-ment

13. _____
14. _____
15. _____
16. _____

Word List

1. joyous
2. useful
3. lonely
4. dangerous
5. hopeful
6. movement
7. playful
8. careless
9. freely
10. painful
11. helpless
12. statement
13. hazardous
14. gladly
15. marvelous
16. fearless
17. treatment
18. suddenly
19. shipment
20. harmless

Challenge Words

21. idly
22. adjustment
23. glamorous

Spelling (continued)

-less

17. _____   18. _____

19. _____   20. _____

Practice B   Write the spelling word next to its meaning clue.

24. full of danger _____

25. without harm _____

26. the result of moving _____

27. in a glad way _____

28. the result of treating _____

29. full of pain _____

30. full of uses _____

31. in a free way _____

32. without help _____

33. in a sudden way _____

34. the result of shipping _____

35. full of hazards _____

Apply   Circle three misspelled words in the sentence below.
Then write each word correctly.

The lonly boy watched a marvelus movie about a playfull porpoise.

36. _____

37. _____

38. _____

Name _____ Date _____

Nouns

Nouns are words that name people, places, things, or ideas.

Rule

- A **common noun** names *any* person, place, thing, or idea.

- A **concrete noun** names something we can touch or see.

- An **abstract noun** names something we cannot touch or see, such as an idea or emotion.

Example

- student, school, chalkboard

- dolphin, girl, water

- friendship, honesty, happiness

Read this paragraph. Look at the words in bold type. Underline the words in bold type that are *concrete* nouns. Circle the words in bold type that are *abstract* nouns.

Robert heard **laughter** as he walked into the **kitchen.** His mother and

brother were baking granola. The **smell** coming from the **oven** was wonderful.

Robert's **stomach** growled as he waited for the **granola** to be done. It was

hard to have **patience!** When the granola was finally ready, Robert showed his

happiness by eating three **bars!**

Capitalization

Focus   Capital letters are used in many places in writing.

Rule	Example
• Capitalize the name of a person, place, or a specific thing.	• Abraham Lincoln, New York, Eiffel Tower
• Capitalize the title of a specific work, such as a book, a movie, a play, or a work of art.	• *Little Women* (book), *Fantasia* (movie), *Cats* (play), *Mona Lisa* (work of art)
• Capitalize the names of months, days, and holidays.	• June, Thursday, Mother's Day

Practice   **Read each sentence. Cross out any word that is not correctly capitalized, and write the correctly capitalized word above it.**

1. egypt is a country in africa.

2. My sister went to new york city to see *the lion king*.

3. I started *treasure island* on friday and finished it on tuesday.

4. James went to visit his dad in arizona for father's day.

5. kelly and shawn have watched *the wizard of oz* nine times.

6. I am going to a new school in franklin in september.

Name _____ Date _____

Prefixes *re-*, *un-*, and *en-*

Focus

A **prefix** is an addition to the beginning of a word. (*un*true)

A **root word** is a word to which a prefix can be added. (un*true*)

The **prefix *re-*** means "again." To *re*view is to view again.

The **prefix *un-*** means "not." If something is *un*fair, it is not fair.

The **prefix *en-*** means "to make a certain way." *En*rich means to make rich.

Practice

Remove the prefixes from the following words, and write the root words on the lines provided.

1. replace _____

2. undependable _____

3. reconsider _____

4. entangle _____

5. unfasten _____

6. recall _____

7. unbelief _____

8. entrust _____

Apply The prefix *re-* means "again." The prefix *un-* means "not." The prefix *en-* means "to make a certain way." Write the meanings of the following words, using the root word and the meaning of the prefix. The first one is done for you.

1. renew <u>to make new again</u>

2. unequal _____

3. unfit _____

4. enlarge _____

5. rewrite _____

6. rebuild _____

Add the prefix *re-*, *un-*, or *en-* to each root word. Then, write each new word in a sentence.

7. consider _____

_____

8. attached _____

_____

9. gain _____

_____

10. educated _____

_____

11. danger _____

_____

12. able _____

_____

Name _____   Date _____

Selection Vocabulary

Focus

hastened (hā' · sənd) *v.* hurried (page 49)

shuddered (shu' · dûrd) *v.* shook with horror (page 49)

despairing (di · spâr' · ing) *adj.* without hope (page 50)

sympathetic (sim' · pə · the' · tik) *adj.* understanding (page 50)

delivered (di · li' · vûrd) *v.* saved (page 51)

flickering (fli' · kûr · ing) *v.* becoming brighter and then darker over and over (page 59)

companion (kəm · pan' · yən) *n.* person who is traveling with someone else (page 59)

concealed (kən · sēld') *v.* hidden (page 61)

Review the vocabulary words and definitions from "Two Tickets to Freedom." Write two sentences that each use at least one of the vocabulary words.

1. _____

_____

2. _____

_____

Apply

Write *T* in the blank if the sentence for the vocabulary word is correct. Write *F* if the sentence is false. For each *F* answer, write the word that fits the definition.

1. *Flickering* is an adjective meaning "without hope."

_____ _____

2. If something is *delivered,* it is hidden.

_____ _____

3. A person who is *sympathetic* is understanding.

_____ _____

4. A *companion* is a person who is traveling with someone else.

_____ _____

5. *Shuddered* means "hurried."

_____ _____

6. A *flickering* light becomes brighter and then darker over and over.

_____ _____

7. If someone is saved from danger, that person is *delivered.*

_____ _____

8. If someone *hastened,* he shook with horror.

_____ _____

Name _____ **Date** _____

Framing Questions to Find Information

"Two Tickets to Freedom" includes topics such as slavery and railroads. Based on the story, fill in the chart with questions about four topics you would like to investigate. Write one question for each topic. Then find answers to your questions either by rereading the selection or by investigating the information in another source.

Questions About a Topic	Information I Found
1.	
2.	

Questions About a Topic	Information I Found
3.	
4.	

Name _____ Date _____

Spelling

Focus

- Remember the prefix *re–* means *again*
- Remember the prefixes *dis–*, and *un–* mean *the opposite of*
- Remember the prefix *mid–* means *in the middle of*

New words can be made by adding one of these prefixes to a root word.

Practice A   **Sort the spelling words under each prefix.**

re–

1. _____
2. _____
3. _____
4. _____
5. _____

dis–

6. _____
7. _____
8. _____
9. _____
10. _____

un–

11. _____
12. _____
13. _____
14. _____
15. _____

mid–

16. _____
17. _____
18. _____
19. _____
20. _____

Word List

1. replace
2. discount
3. review
4. unfold
5. midterm
6. rewind
7. unfair
8. midlife
9. displace
10. untie
11. renew
12. undone
13. disown
14. reheat
15. midnight
16. uncover
17. midwest
18. disagree
19. midway
20. disappear

Challenge Words

21. dissolve
22. rearrange
23. unfamiliar

Spelling (continued)

Practice B Write the spelling word next to its meaning clue.

24. in the middle of life _____

25. to view again _____

26. the opposite of fold _____

27. the opposite of agree _____

28. to heat again _____

29. in the middle of the night _____

30. the opposite of own _____

31. the opposite of cover _____

32. to wind again _____

33. the opposite of place _____

34. the opposite of tie _____

35. the opposite of fair _____

Apply Circle the words that are spelled correctly.

36. reknew   renoo   renew

37. middwest   Midwest   midwist

38. disappeat   disappear   disapear

Name _____ **Date** _____

Action Verbs

Focus

An **action verb** shows what the subject does. The action can be seen or unseen.
Example: Molly **thought** about her idea.

hopped	read	erupted
broke	found	constructed
climbs	saved	swings
ran	spins	

Practice **Fill in the blank with the correct action verb.**

1. Ilana _____ down the hallway as fast as she could.

2. Jupiter _____ faster than Earth.

3. A volcano _____ just miles away from our island resort.

4. Sam _____ up and down on one foot.

5. She _____ a bird feeder out of craft sticks.

6. He _____ higher than anyone else.

7. Hannah _____ her arm in two places.

8. Our teacher _____ *Beauty and the Beast* to us.

Exact Words

Focus

Good writers use **exact words** to express things and actions clearly and to help readers understand their writing. General words do not create pictures the way exact words do.

Read the two examples, and notice how much more interesting the second sentence is.

Sentence with General Words
He opened the door.

Sentence with Exact Words
He slowly pushed open the heavy creaking door.

Practice

Each sentence below contains general words. Replace general words with exact words, or add exact words to improve each sentence. Write your new sentence in the space provided. Remember to think about the picture you want to create in your readers' minds.

1. She walked into the office.

_____

2. I bounced a ball on the sidewalk.

_____

3. The trees were pretty.

_____

4. The cat looked at the dog.

_____

5. The room was full of stuff.

_____

Name _____ Date _____

Suffixes -y, -ful, and -less

Focus

The **suffix -y** means "being, having." Examples:
rain*y* = having rain; funn*y* = being fun

The **suffix -ful** means "full of." Example: cheer*ful* = full of cheer

The **suffix -less** means "without." Example: pain*less* = without pain

Note: When adding -y to a word, if the word has one syllable and ends with a short vowel and consonant, double the final consonant before adding -y.

Example: *(fun, funny)*

Practice   Add the suffix -y, -ful, or -less to each boldfaced word so that it matches the definition given.

1. full of **play** _____

2. having **sun** _____

3. without **hope** _____

4. being **summer** _____

5. without **use** _____

6. not able to **rest** _____

7. full of **help** _____

8. without a **home** _____

9. having **web** _____

10. full of **joy** _____

Apply | Complete each sentence with the correct form of each word.

11. I thought my teacher was (fault, faultless), but then she made a mistake.

12. I hope tomorrow will be a (sun, sunny) day.

13. You will have to take good (care, careful) of your new pet.

14. Mandie was (thank, thankful) that her dad got home from work early.

15. The newborn baby was quite (helpful, helpless). She couldn't do anything for herself.

16. He got rid of his old computer because it was (useful, useless).

Add the suffix *-y, -ful,* or *-less* to each root word. Then, write each new word in a sentence.

17. skill _____

_____

18. thought _____

_____

19. cheer _____

_____

20. pain _____

_____

Name _____ Date _____

Selection Vocabulary

Focus

merriment (mâr'·i·mənt) *n.* fun (page 72)

tangled (tang'·gəld) *v.* twisted together or snarled (page 75)

miserable (mi'·zûr·bəl) *adj.* very unhappy (page 75)

obviously (ob'·vē·əs·lē) *adv.* in a way that is easy to see (page 76)

recalled (ri·käld') *v.* remembered (page 76)

gnawing (nô'·ing) *v.* chewing (page 78)

cover (ku'·vûr) *n.* something that would be good to hide behind (page 79)

circumstances (sûr·cəm·stans·əs) *n.* the way things are at the moment (page 80)

Practice Fill in the blank with a vocabulary word from this lesson to complete each sentence.

1. The boys _____ the cords when they put away the tools.

2. Grandfather used a plastic _____ to protect the fishing boat.

3. There was _____ at the party.

4. Anne was _____ after she broke her leg.

5. The beaver's large teeth are perfect for _____ on tree limbs.

6. The smiling father was _____ proud of his son's talents.

7. Carlos laughed as he _____ the first time he tried to ride a bike.

8. Under the _____ Kellie did the best with what she had.

Apply Write the word from the word box that matches each description below.

cover	miserable	obviously	gnawing
merriment	tangled	circumstances	recalled

1. _____ wrapped in a mess of strings

2. _____ a good place to stay out of view

3. _____ happiness

4. _____ easily seen

5. _____ brought to mind

6. _____ biting or nibbling

7. _____ very sad

8. _____ the state of things at the moment

Write a sentence using at least one of the vocabulary words from this lesson.

_____

_____

_____

_____

Name _____ Date _____

Cause and Effect

Practice

Look through "Mrs. Frisby and the Crow" for examples of cause-and-effect relationships. For each example, write the event that is the cause and the event that is the effect.

1. Cause: _____

_____

Effect: _____

_____

2. Cause: _____

_____

Effect: _____

_____

Practice

Rewrite each pair of sentences as one sentence showing the cause-and-effect relationship.

3. I could not eat dinner. I ate all the apples.

_____

_____

4. Scruffy bit me. I've been afraid of dogs.

_____

_____

5. I could not find my shoes. I was late.

_____

_____

6. Rachel and Jose put in too much sugar. The recipe did not work.

_____

_____

Apply

Think about a machine you see every day. Write down how you think it works, using cause-and-effect signal words.

_____

_____

_____

_____

Name _____ Date _____

Taking Notes

Taking notes means writing down information from investigation sources. Good notes contain key phrases and short sentences that sum up important facts and ideas. When taking notes, follow these guidelines:

- Create subject headings and use them to organize your notes.

- Include only the most important information on the topic.

- Write notes in your own words.

- Keep your notes short. Use abbreviations and key phrases that you will recognize.

Write the name of your topic for your investigation. Look through some of the resources you have chosen for your investigation, such as an almanac or magazine. Select two and write notes from these resources. Create subheadings for your notes to help you organize and classify different types of information.

The title of my topic is: _____

1. Resource title:

_____

_____

Notes:

_____

_____

_____

_____

_____

2. Resource title:

_____

_____

Notes:

_____

_____

_____

_____

_____

_____

_____

_____

_____

_____

_____

_____

_____

_____

_____

_____

_____

_____

_____

_____

_____

Name _____ Date _____

Writing a Biography

Think Audience: **Who** will read this biography?

_____

Purpose: **What** do you want your readers to think about your subject?

_____

Prewriting After you collect information on your subject, use this graphic organizer to plan your biography. Remember that the main idea is the most important point, and the details support the main idea.

Subject

Main Idea	Main Idea	Main Idea

1. _____   1. _____   1. _____

_____   _____   _____

_____   _____   _____

2. _____   2. _____   2. _____

_____   _____   _____

_____   _____   _____

Conclusion

Revising

Use this checklist to revise your biography. You can ask your teacher or another classmate to read your biography and complete the checklist too.

☐ Do you tell the important parts of your subject's life?

☐ Are the events in your subject's life presented in chronological order?

☐ Do your words describe how your subject really is/was?

☐ Did you use multiple sources to cross-check information?

Editing/Proofreading

Use this checklist to correct mistakes.

☐ Make sure that all words are correctly spelled.

☐ Check all punctuation to make sure it is correct.

☐ Make sure each proper noun begins with a capital letter.

Publishing

Use this checklist to prepare for publication.

☐ Print out or write a neat final copy.

☐ Include photographs with your biography.

Name _____ Date _____

Spelling

Focus

- The spelling of base words may change when **affixes** are added.

- Words ending in a silent e usually drop the e before adding the suffix that begins with a vowel.

- The base word solve plus the affix –able is formed when the silent e is dropped and able is added to create *solvable*. Drop the silent e at the end of base words when adding a suffix that begins with a vowel.

- For base words that end in y and are preceded by a consonant, change the y to an i when adding a suffix that begins with a vowel.

- Some words require special changes. For example, when adding –ly to adjectives that end in c, add –ally instead).

Word List

1. angrily
2. location
3. promotion
4. famous
5. precision
6. basically
7. memorable
8. easily
9. conclusion
10. solvable
11. erosion
12. attention
13. decision
14. usable
15. courteous
16. envious
17. gracious
18. luckily
19. flammable
20. pollution

Challenge Words

21. wondrous
22. miserable
23. terrifically

Practice A Write the spelling word for each base word.

1. angry _____
2. basic _____
3. easy _____
4. lucky _____
5. locate _____
6. promote _____
7. attend _____
8. pollute _____
9. precise _____
10. conclude _____
11. erode _____
12. decide _____
13. fame _____
14. courtesy _____
15. envy _____
16. grace _____

Spelling (continued)

17. memory _____   20. flame _____   22. wonder _____

18. solve _____   **Challenge Words**   23. misery _____

19. use _____   21. terrific _____

Practice B   **Use your knowledge of the meanings of affixes to decide which spelling word makes the most sense in each blank below. Write the spelling word on the line.**

24. My boss promoted me. I received a _____.

25. Chuck looked at me in an angry way. He stared at me _____.

26. An actor having fame signed his picture. That person is _____.

27. She was able to solve the mystery. The mystery was _____.

28. Wind can erode the soil. _____ changes the landscape.

29. Dad is able to use this broken tool. It remains _____.

30. What did you conclude? What _____ did you reach?

31. Mrs. Diamond spoke in an easy way. She talked _____ to the class.

32. Please locate Dallas on the map. Describe its _____.

33. The babysitter is full of courtesy. Her actions are _____.

Apply   **Circle the words that are spelled correctly.**

34. envyous   envious   envous

35. pollution   polution   pollushun

36. desision   dicision   decision

37. luckly   luckily   luckally

38. memmorable   memorible   memorable

Name _____ Date _____

Linking Verbs

Focus

A **linking verb** does not show action. Linking verbs connect the subject of a sentence with a noun or adjective that renames or describes the subject.

Example: Austin **is** a very good golfer.

In the sentence above, the linking verb = **is**. It links the words **Austin** and **golfer**.

Practice

Each of the following sentences contains a linking verb. Circle the linking verb in each sentence. Then draw an arrow from the subject of the sentence to the noun or adjective it is connected to by the linking verb.

1. The new teacher seems kind.

2. Scientists are still confused about the results of the experiment.

3. Your dog is quite large.

4. The two friends were inseparable.

5. Jeffrey was hungry after a long day.

6. My mom is pleased with my grades this quarter.

7. Justin looks really sad today.

8. I am a student at West Creek Elementary.

Verb Phrases

An **action verb** shows what the subject does.
Example: Angela **danced** in the school program.

A **helping verb** helps the main verb.
Example: Angela **will** dance in the school program.

A **verb phrase** is the main verb and helping verb together.
Example: Angela **is dancing** in the school program.

In some cases, the main verb and helping verb are not next to each other in the sentence.
Example: She **could** not **leave** the foolish crow there.

The following paragraphs contain several verb phrases. Circle each verb phrase. Underline the helping verb. Double underline the main verb.

Danny and Paul were walking their dogs in the park. It was their favorite way to spend Saturday mornings. The day was beautiful.

"Which path should we take?" Danny asked.

There were three paths. They usually took the longest one.

"We could try a new path this time," said Paul.

They did take the new path. It quickly became their favorite trail.

Name _____ Date _____

Verb Endings -*ed* and -*ing*

Focus

The -*ed* **ending** shows past tense.

For words ending in *e*, drop the e before adding -*ed*. (*practice, practiced*)

For words ending in short vowel plus consonant, double the final consonant before adding -*ed*. (*nap, napped; hum, hummed*)

The -*ing* **ending** shows that something is happening right now.

For words ending in *e*, drop the e before adding -*ing*. (*practice, practicing*)

For words ending in short vowel plus *p*, short vowel plus *t*, or short vowel plus *m*, double the final consonant before adding -*ing*. (*nap, napping; hit, hitting*)

Practice   **Circle the correct word in parentheses.**

1. She (skidded, skided) to a stop on her skateboard.

2. They (raced, racing) to the end of the street and back.

3. She has been (hopping, hoping) on one foot for nearly a minute.

4. Colin and Anna are (dropped, dropping) their dogs off at my house.

5. The baby (napped, naped) for a while and woke up refreshed.

6. What tune is Tara (hummed, humming)?

7. My dog is (biting, bitting) his new bone.

8. Paula (slammed, slamming) her books down on the table.

Plurals

Plurals are words that mean "more than one."

An s can be added to the singular form of a noun to form a plural (*cat* becomes *cats*).

Add -es to words that end in *sh, ch, ss, s,* and *x* to form plurals (*bushes, matches, messes, buses, boxes*).

In words that end with consonant -*y*, the *y* is changed to *i* before -es is added (*baby, babies; cry, cries*).

Practice   **Write the plural form of the following words.**

1. number _____

2. tax _____

3. smudge _____

4. cliff _____

5. dollar _____

6. ferry _____

7. arrow _____

8. monkey _____

9. leash _____

10. country _____

Name _____ Date _____

Selection Vocabulary

Focus

tensely (tents'·lē) *adv.* feeling emotional strain (page 91)

pleading (plē'·ding) *v.* begging (page 93)

paces (pā'·səz) *v.* walks back and forth (page 93)

opportunities (o'·pûr·tōō'· nə·tēz) *n.* chances to succeed in life (page 93)

decent (dē'·sənt) *adj.* good enough to make someone comfortable (page 97)

stable (stā'·bəl) *adj.* steady, dependable (page 98)

concerned (kən·sûrnd') *v.* showing worry (page 99)

strive (strīv) *v.* work to get something (page 100)

Practice
Write the vocabulary word that best matches the underlined word or phrase in the sentences below.

1. Kate and her brother argued <u>feeling emotional strain.</u>

   _____

2. Will your pay at the store be <u>good enough to make you comfortable?</u>

   _____

3. Your dad was <u>showing worry</u> when you did not come home on time.

   _____

4. My horse <u>walks back and forth</u> just like I do when I am nervous.

   _____

5. I look forward to many great <u>chances to succeed in life</u>.

   _____

6. You should always <u>work</u> to do your best. _____

Apply **Circle the correct word that completes each sentence.**

7. Rachel is _____ that the package will not arrive on time.

   a. concerned   **b.** strive   **c.** pleading

8. Danny is _____ with his sister to share her candy with him.

   a. decent   **b.** pleading   **c.** stable

9. i listened _____ as my two best friends argued back and forth.

   a. tensely   **b.** strive   **c.** opportunities

10. If you _____ for an A on your test, I know you can do it.

   a. stable   **b.** concerned   **c.** strive

11. A college education will give you many _____ for a good job.

   a. paces   **b.** decent   **c.** opportunities

12. Ian is hoping to earn a _____ amount of money this summer.

   a. decent   **b.** concerned   **c.** paces

13. Laura's father _____ the length of his workshop when he's deep in thought.

   a. pleading   **b.** paces   **c.** pleading

14. Her career will definitely provide a _____ future for her family.

   a. stable   **b.** concerned   **c.** strive

Name _____ Date _____

Author's Purpose

Focus The **author's purpose** is the main reason for presenting a story or selection in a certain way. An author's purpose

- can be to *inform*, to *explain*, to *entertain*, or to *persuade*.
- affects things in the story, such as the *details, descriptions, story events,* and *dialogue.*

An author can have more than one purpose for writing.

Practice A **Read each paragraph below. Pay attention to details and story events. Then write the author's purpose: to inform, to explain, to entertain, or to persuade.**

1. I thought balancing a gumdrop on my nose was a pretty good idea. What I didn't know was that the gumdrop had just fallen off my sister's gingerbread house. It had fresh glue on it. I balanced it all the way through two songs on the radio. I think I invented a new dance!

   Purpose: _____

2. If the Elm Street playground is closed, hundreds of families will be affected. Children need a safe place to play. Without the playground they will be forced to use sidewalks and streets for their games. We cannot let the playground be closed.

   Purpose: _____

Practice B Read the title of each story below. Then write what the author's purpose might be for writing the story—to *inform*, to *explain*, to *entertain*, or to *persuade*.

3. *The Dog That Ate New York*

Author's purpose: _____

4. *Water Safety for Swimming-Pool Owners*

Author's purpose: _____

5. *The Care and Feeding of Mice*

Author's purpose: _____

6. *Why You Should Vote*

Author's purpose: _____

7. *My Mother, the Time Traveler*

Author's purpose: _____

Apply Write your own paragraph with the purpose of *informing* your readers of something.

_____

_____

_____

_____

_____

_____

Name _____ Date _____

Maps and Atlases

Map A

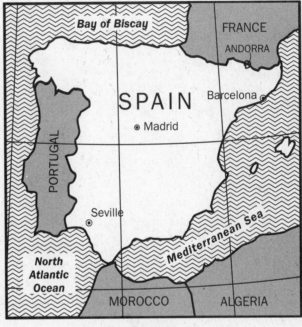

Map B

Write four questions about either Map A or Map B. Give your questions to a classmate. When your classmate has finished answering them, discuss the questions. Share how maps could be useful in your research project for this or other units.

1. _____

_____

2. _____

_____

3. _____

_____

4. _____

_____

In the box, draw a map of one of the following: your city/town, your state, or your region of the country. Use a map or atlas to help you accurately plot cities, landforms, or landmarks. Draw a scale that shows how many miles are represented by inches on your map. Then write five questions about your map for a classmate to answer. Discuss the questions together.

1.

2.

3.

4.

5.

Name _____ **Date** _____

Writing a Play with Fantasy Elements

Think

Audience: Who will read your fantasy play?

_____

Purpose: What is your reason for writing a fantasy play?

_____

Prewriting

Use this graphic organizer to plan your play. Remember that a fantasy should have elements of suspense and surprise.

Setting

Characters

Plot

Scenes and Stage Directions

Dialogue

Revising

Use this checklist to revise your play.

☐ Does your main character match the description you created in your character sketch?

☐ Are parts of your play suspenseful and surprising?

☐ Does your dialogue keep the story moving?

☐ Did you vary the types of sentences in the dialogue so that the characters sound realistic?

Editing/Proofreading

Use this checklist to correct mistakes.

☐ Did you check all words for correct spelling?

☐ Did you check all punctuation to make sure that it is correct?

☐ Do your sentences and proper nouns begin with capital letters?

Publishing

Use this checklist to prepare for publication.

☐ Write or type a neat final copy.

☐ Read your work one more time. Correct any errors.

Spelling

Name _____   Date _____

Focus

- The spelling of base words may change in predictable ways when **inflectional endings** are added.
- For many base words, simply add the inflectional endings.
- Drop *silent e* before adding *–ed* and *–ing*.
- When a word ends in *consonant-y*, change the *y* to *i* and add the ending.
- Double the final consonant before adding the endings *–ed* and *–ing* to words that contain a short vowel sound.

Word List

1. pleading
2. building
3. painting
4. finished
5. worried
6. unplugged
7. opening
8. insisted
9. controlled
10. leaving
11. danced
12. shedding
13. rating
14. striped
15. stripped
16. fitting
17. ringing
18. setting
19. bleached
20. curved

Challenge Words

21. concerned
22. beginning
23. preoccupied

Practice A   Write the spelling word for each base word. Finish writing the rule that applies to each group of words on the line below each group.

1. plead _____

2. build _____

3. paint _____

4. finish _____

5. worry _____

6. unplug _____

7. open _____

8. insist _____

9. control _____

10. leave _____

Spelling (continued)

Rule: When a word ends in consonant-y, change the y to i and add the ending.

11. dance _____

12. shed _____

13. rate _____

14. stripe _____

15. strip _____

Rule: Double the final consonant before adding the endings -ed and -ing to words that contain a short vowel sound.

16. fit _____

17. ring _____

18. set _____

19. bleach _____

20. curve _____

Rule: Drop silent e before adding -ed and -ing

Apply

Decide which spelling word completes each thought in this paragraph. Then write those spelling words on the lines provided.

Bells were ri_____ as the couple left the church. They were le_____ on a trip to Greece. The groom began shed_____ his stri_____ tuxedo jacket, while the bride admired the diamond set_____ in her ring once again. Mr. and Mrs. Morrow looked forward to seeing a famous pai_____ in Athens.

21. _____

22. _____

23. _____

24. _____

25. _____

26. _____

Name _____ Date _____

Personal Object Pronouns

Focus

A **pronoun** is used in place of one or more nouns.

Like nouns, pronouns can be subjects or objects in a sentence.

A pronoun that receives the action of the verb is the direct object. (The cat chased **it.**)

A pronoun after a preposition is the object of the preposition. (The bird flew over **me.**)

Personal pronouns name specific people or things.

Personal object pronouns are *me, you, him, her, it, us, you,* and *them.*

Practice

In each of the following sentences, the object is underlined. On the line, write a personal object pronoun to replace the noun(s).

1. Kerry was born before <u>James</u>. _____

2. I lost <u>my wallet</u> at the amusement park. _____

3. I wanted to tell <u>Claire and Lola</u> the good news. _____

4. Viv was nervous about reading her paper to <u>Phoebe and me</u>. _____

5. The two girls sat down beside <u>Mrs. Gibbon</u>. _____

6. I read <u>the whole book</u> in one day. _____

Dialogue and Direct Speech

Focus

When characters in a story talk, their conversation is called **dialogue.** Dialogue is also a way to reveal details about characters. Good dialogue makes a story more interesting. **Direct speech** is like dialogue and is often used in expository writing.

Rule

- Each character's exact words are enclosed in quotation marks.

- Usually, a new paragraph begins each time the speaker changes.

- Punctuation for dialogue goes inside quotation marks.

- Speaker tags, such as *said Ben* and *Katie pouted* must be used often enough for readers to keep track of who is speaking.

Example

"I don't think Syd likes me anymore," Katie pouted. "She never stays to talk to me after school."

"Oh, Katie, didn't you know?" said Ben. "Her mom has been really sick. She just got out of the hospital."

Practice

Rewrite each sentence or set of sentences as dialogue. Capitalize, indent, and punctuate your dialogue correctly.

1. I told Ron that I couldn't help him. _____

_____

_____

2. Ruth said we must have mushrooms on the pizza. Eric told Ruth

he is allergic to mushrooms. _____

_____

Grammar, Usage, and Mechanics • *Skills Practice 1*

Name _____ Date _____

Compounds

> **Focus**
>
> A **compound word** is a word that is made up of two or more smaller words. *(playmate, timetable)*
>
> A word with a prefix or suffix is not compound. *(unfair, played)*
>
> **Compounds** can be open, closed, or hyphenated.
>
> An **open compound** is two separate words. Example: **high school**
>
> A **closed compound** is combined into one word. Example: **loudspeaker**
>
> A **hyphenated compound** connects two words with a hyphen. Example: **first-class**
>
> Use a dictionary to find out if a compound word is **open, closed,** or **hyphenated.**

Practice A

Write the following sets of words as compounds. Read the clue in parentheses to find out how to write the word correctly.

1. warm, blooded (hyphenated) _____

2. birth, day (closed) _____

3. tail, gate (closed) _____

4. trash, can (open) _____

5. billy, goat (open) _____

6. empty, handed (hyphenated) _____

7. clean, cut (hyphenated) _____

8. ship, wreck (closed) _____

Practice B Circle the compound word in each sentence. On the line, write what kind of compound it is (open, closed, or hyphenated).

9. When I hurt my arm, it took a lot of self-control to keep from crying.

_____

10. Is there a difference between a hedgehog and a porcupine?

_____

11. We always have to return our textbooks at the end of the year.

_____

12. There was a sweet-smelling scent coming from the bakery on the corner.

_____

13. My favorite player hit a grand slam last night to win the game.

_____

14. Gaige can jump like a grasshopper. _____

15. When it comes to gardening, my aunt has a green thumb.

_____

Apply Write a sentence using each of the following compound words.

16. **firstborn** _____

17. **honeycomb** _____

_____

18. **empty-handed** _____

_____

19. **sixty-six** _____

Name _____ Date _____

Selection Vocabulary

Focus

brilliant (bril'·yənt) *adj.* bright (page 110)

spread (spred) *v.* open outward (page 110)

luxurious (lug'·zhŏŏr'·ē·əs) *adj.* rich and comfortable (page 110)

plunged (plunjd) *v.* fell (page 113)

nudged (nujd) *v.* pushed slightly (page 113)

crowed (krōd) *v.* bragged loudly (page 113)

astonishment (ə·sto'·nish·mənt) *n.* sudden wonder (page 113)

Practice Write the vocabulary word next to the group of words that have a similar meaning.

1. unfold; open; unroll _____

2. wonder; amazement; surprise _____

3. dipped; fell; submerged _____

4. prodded; poked; pushed _____

5. lush; rich; abundant _____

6. boasted; bragged; flaunted _____

7. sparkling; bright; radiant _____

Apply   **Write the word that best fits each clue below.**

8. Someone was proud of an accomplishment and told everyone about it.

What did he do? _____

9. A person might have this reaction to a surprise birthday party.

What is it? _____

10. The stars are sparkling and shining brightly tonight.

What are they? _____

11. The fabric on the new chair was made of soft, expensive velvet.

What was it? _____

12. Baby birds must do this to their wings when they are learning to fly.

What is it? _____

13. Josiah gently pushed his sister forward in line.

What did he do to her? _____

14. Teron dove into the pool.

What is another word for what he did? _____

Writing an Advertisement

Think

Audience: Who is the audience for your advertisement?

_____

Purpose: What do you want your readers to think about your product?

_____

Prewriting

One way to convince readers to buy a product or service is to show a cause-and-effect relationship. Use the cause-and-effect map below to organize your ideas for your advertisement.

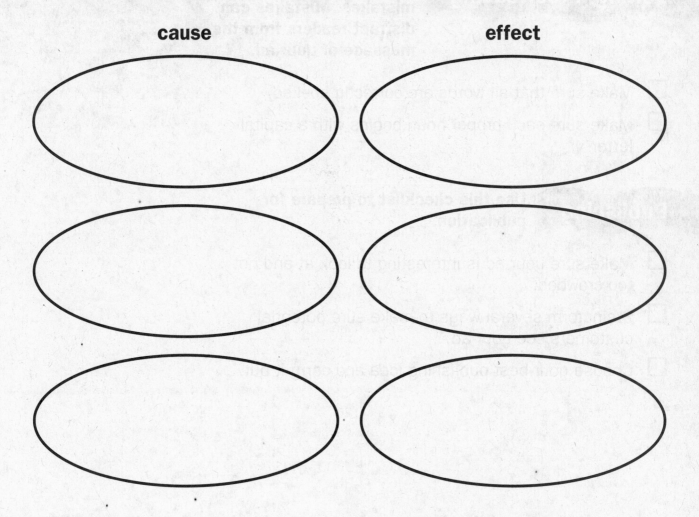

cause   effect

Revising

Use this checklist to make sure your ad is as convincing as possible.

☐ Did you give the most convincing reasons to buy your product or service?

☐ Did you focus your ad on the needs of your audience?

☐ Is your ad full of energy and excitement?

☐ Did you arrange your words to grab the readers' attention?

Editing/Proofreading

Use this checklist to correct mistakes. Mistakes can distract readers from the message of your ad.

☐ Make sure that all words are correctly spelled.

☐ Make sure each proper noun begins with a capital letter.

Publishing

Use this checklist to prepare for publication.

☐ Make sure your ad is interesting to look at and not too crowded.

☐ Brainstorm several ways to make sure potential customers see your ad.

☐ Choose your best publishing idea and carry it out.

Name _____ Date _____

Spelling

Focus

- **Compound words** are formed by joining together two words. Some words that make up compound words may have one or more syllables.

- Sometimes compound words combine the meanings of the two smaller words they contain.

Practice A Combine each pair of smaller words to write a compound word. Then softly pronounce each spelling word and write the number of syllables you hear.

1. coast + line = _____ ____

2. sun + screen = _____ ____

3. when + ever = _____ ____

4. high + way = _____ ____

5. head + line = _____ ____

6. flash + light = _____ ____

7. any + one = _____ ____

8. some + times = _____ ____

9. door + bell = _____ ____

10. no + where = _____ ____

11. shell + fish = _____ ____

12. eye + sight = _____ ____

13. world + wide = _____ ____

Word List
1. highway
2. flashlight
3. basketball
4. anyone
5. headline
6. sometimes
7. shellfish
8. doorbell
9. eyesight
10. handlebar
11. worldwide
12. outline
13. footprint
14. waterfall
15. brainstorm
16. nowhere
17. whenever
18. sunscreen
19. homework
20. coastline

Challenge Words
21. motorcycle
22. toothache
23. wristwatch

Spelling (continued)

14. out + line = _____ ____

15. foot + print = _____ ____

16. water + fall = _____ ____

17. brain + storm = _____ ____

18. basket + ball = _____ ____

Apply Compound words do not always combine the meanings of the smaller words they contain. Write the spelling words that go with these silly definitions. The first one is done for you.

19. when it rains brains _____

20. a way that is higher than others _____

21. a line that is out of bounds _____

22. any flashing light _____

23. a ball made out of a basket _____

24. a line that coasts downhill _____

Name _____ Date _____

Complete Subjects and Predicates

The **simple subject** of a sentence is a *noun* that tells *whom* or *what* the sentence is about.

The **simple predicate** of a sentence is a *verb* that tells what the subject *does.*

The **complete subject** includes all the words that describe the subject.

The **complete predicate** includes all the words that follow the predicate.

Example: The brilliantly-colored lorikeet landed on her shoulder.

Simple subject = lorikeet

Simple predicate = landed

Complete subject = The brilliantly-colored lorikeet

Complete predicate = landed on her shoulder

In each of the following sentences, draw a line between the complete subject and the complete predicate. Circle the simple subject. Underline the simple predicate. The first one is done for you.

1. My favorite ⟨teacher⟩/<u>moved</u> to Alabama last month.

2. Her dad's birthday present arrived in the mail this morning.

3. Patrick's entire family played in the flag football game at the reunion.

4. The twinkling stars shone brightly in the summer sky.

5. Denny's new puppy barked all night long.

6. Zoe's old bedroom is now an office.

Practice B — In each of the following sentences, circle the complete subject and underline the complete predicate.

7. An excited Daniel rushed into the room to see his big birthday gift.

8. The happy puppy dug a deep hole for her bone.

9. The rowdy class rushed through the doors to the Aquarium.

10. The noisy owl flapped his wings all night.

11. An anxious patient waited nervously for the doctor to call him.

12. The crazy cat climbed the huge tree for the third time despite getting stuck.

Apply — Write two sentences, circle the simple subject and the simple predicate, and underline the complete subject and the complete predicate.

_____

_____

_____

_____

Greek Roots

Focus English words also contain parts, or roots, that have been borrowed from the ancient language of Greek. When you know the meaning of a **Greek root,** you can begin to figure out the meaning of the English word that contains it. Here are some common Greek roots and their meanings:

micro = small	*tele* = far off	*graph* = to write
bio = life	*geo* = earth	*astr* = star
log = word	*phon* = sounds	

The word *telephone* has the Greek roots **tele** and **phon,** which mean "far off" and "sounds." You can tell from the meaning of the Greek roots that a telephone is a device that allows you to hear sounds from far off.

Practice A Read the following Greek roots and their meanings. Write another word containing each Greek root beside the one provided.

1. *meter:* "measure"; centimeter _____

2. *cycl:* "circle"; tricycle _____

3. *astr:* "star"; astronomy _____

4. *micro:* "small"; microscope _____

5. *graph:* "to write"; telegraph _____

Practice B The following groups of words all have the same Greek roots. Circle the root that each word has in common. Then examine each word carefully and think of its meaning. Think about what the meanings have in common. Then choose a definition for the root from the box below and write it in the blank.

heat	word	to see	to write

6. diagram: a plan or sketch
   telegram: a message
   grammar: rules about writing

   The Greek root is *gram*. What does *gram* mean? _____

7. telescope: allows you to see distant things
   microscope: allows you to see tiny things
   periscope: allows you to see above the water
   while in a submarine

   The Greek root is *scop*. What does *scop* mean? _____

8. thermos: keeps liquids hot
   thermometer: measures how hot or cold something is
   thermostat: controls the heater

   The Greek root is *therm*. What does *therm* mean? _____

9. dialogue: words exchanged between people
   monologue: a speech given by a single person in a play
   apology: words spoken to say you are sorry

   The Greek root is *log*. What does *log* mean? _____

Name _____ Date _____

Selection Vocabulary

Focus

jagged (ja'•gəd) *adj.* having sharp points that stick out (page 136)

trickled (tri'•kəld) *v.* past tense of **trickle:** to run slowly in a series of drops or a thin stream (page 137)

flowed (flōd) *v.* past tense form of **flow:** to move as water does (page 137)

raging (ra'•jing) *adj.* violent, wild (page 138)

irrigation (ēr'•ə•gā'•shən) *adj.* having to do with supplying farmland with water (page 139)

reservoir (re'•zə•vwär') *n.* a lake for storing water (page 140)

particles (pär'•ti•kəlz) *n.* plural form of **particle:** a tiny piece (page 140)

glacier (glā'•shûr) *n.* a huge mass of ice formed from unmelted snow, usually found in the polar regions or high mountains (page 144)

Practice A **Write the vocabulary word that best matches the underlined word or phrase in the sentences below.**

1. I took a picture of the <u>huge mass of ice</u> from our ship's window.

_____

2. The stream <u>moved as water does</u> down the mountain. _____

3. They walked around the <u>lake that stores water</u> three times.

_____

4. The mountain had several <u>sharp-pointed</u> peaks. _____

5. The water <u>ran slowly</u> out of the faucet. _____

6. The new <u>water-supplying</u> system on my uncle's farm uses advanced

technology. _____

Practice B Write the word from the word box that matches each definition below.

| jagged | particles | flowed | reservoir |
| trickled | glacier | irrigation | raging |

1. _____ a huge piece of slowly moving, compacted snow

2. _____ a large reserve of water

3. _____ moved freely

4. _____ flowed in droplets

5. _____ fierce, intense

6. _____ watering crops or land artificially

7. _____ small pieces of solid matter

8. _____ having pointed, sharp notches

Apply Write a sentence using at least one of the vocabulary words from this lesson.

Name _____ Date _____

Sequence

Focus

Sequence is the order of events in a story. Writers often use signal words called time-and-order words to help readers follow the action in a story.

Time-and-order words show

- the **order** in which events take place. Words such as *first, then, so, when,* and *finally* show order.

- the passage of **time** in a story. Words such as *spring, tomorrow,* and *morning* show time.

Practice A

Look through "The Snowflake: A Water Cycle Story." Find sentences with time and order words. Write the words along with a *T* next to the word if it shows time or an *O* if it shows order. Then explain how these words help you understand the sequence of events in the story.

1. Word: _____ Time/Order _____

2. Word: _____ Time/Order _____

3. Word: _____ Time/Order _____

4. Word: _____ Time/Order _____

5. Word: _____ Time/Order _____

How do these words help you understand the sequence of events in the story?

_____

_____

Practice B   Read the following passages. In the first passage, fill in the spaces with words that signal time. In the second passage, fill in the spaces with words that signal order.

_____ the bank is open from 9:00 A.M. to 5:00 P.M.

It closes at 3:00 P.M. _____ .

_____ is a holiday, so the bank will be closed all day.

The _____ stop on the tour was the old Post Office.

_____ we visited the theater.

_____ lunch we saw the library.

_____ we visited the museum.

Apply   Write a short paragraph about an ordinary day in your life. Use time and order words in your paragraph.

_____

_____

_____

_____

_____

_____

_____

_____

_____

Name _____ Date _____

Parts of a Book

Understanding the parts of a book will help you find information faster because you will know where to look. Some books, but not all, have these parts.

These pages are at the front of many books.

- The **title page** gives the title of the book, the names of the author or editor and the illustrator, and the name of the publisher.

- The **copyright page** gives the publisher's name and the place and year the book was published.

- The **table of contents** lists, in numerical order, the units, chapters, or stories in the book with the page number on which each item begins.

These pages are at the back of many books.

- The **index** is an alphabetical list in the back of the book of important names and subjects and the pages on which they appear.

- The **bibliography** is a list of books, newspapers, magazines, and other resources that the author used for information.

- The **glossary** is an alphabetical list of special words used in the book and their definitions.

Use books from the library or your classroom to answer these questions.

1. Complete the following about a fiction book that contains this information.

Title: _____

Author: _____

Illustrator: _____

Copyright date: _____

Where can you find the name of the publisher? _____

_____

Where can you find a list of the units and chapter titles in a book?

_____

2. **Complete the following about a nonfiction book that contains this information**

Title: _____

Copyright date: _____

Author(s) or Editor(s): _____

Illustrator or Photographer: _____

What is the title of the first chapter? _____

The first chapter begins on which page? _____

Based on the chapter title, what is Chapter 1 about? _____

_____

These four entries and page numbers are listed in the index.

_____

_____

_____

These four words and their meanings are from the glossary.

_____

_____

_____

Name _____ Date _____

Describing How to Do Something

Think

Audience: Who is the audience for your description?

_____

Purpose: What is your reason for writing a description?

_____

Prewriting

Use this graphic organizer to write the steps in the process you are explaining. Write the steps in the correct sequence.

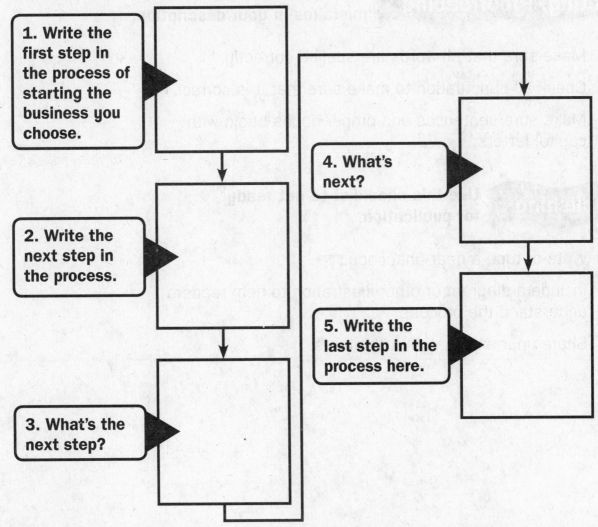

1. Write the first step in the process of starting the business you choose.

2. Write the next step in the process.

3. What's the next step?

4. What's next?

5. Write the last step in the process here.

Revising
Use this checklist to revise your description.

☐ Is each step clearly written?

☐ Have you left out any important steps or information?

☐ Did you include words that show the order of the steps?

☐ Do you explain why this process is important to readers?

☐ Have you revised to eliminate any irrelevant information?

Editing/Proofreading
Use this checklist to correct mistakes in your description.

☐ Make sure that all words are spelled correctly.

☐ Check all punctuation to make sure that it is correct.

☐ Make sure sentences and proper nouns begin with capital letters.

Publishing
Use this checklist to get ready for publication.

☐ Write or type a neat final copy.

☐ Include a diagram or other illustration to help readers understand the process.

☐ Share your explanation with others.

Name _____   **Date** _____

Greek Roots

Focus

Many English words contain **Greek roots**. If you know the spellings and meanings of common Greek roots, you can figure out how to spell and define words that contain them.

- The Greek root *phon* means sound.
- The Greek root *demos* means people.
- The Greek root *path* means feeling.
- The Greek root *derm* means skin.
- The Greek root *historia* means learning or knowing.
- The Greek root kardia (or cardia) means heart.

Word List

1. telephone
2. phonic
3. microphone
4. homophone
5. democracy
6. pandemic
7. demography
8. academy
9. pathos
10. pathetic
11. empathy
12. dermis
13. epidermis
14. dermatology
15. history
16. historian
17. historic
18. prehistoric
19. cardiac
20. cardiology

Challenge Words:

21. cacophony
22. symphony
23. sympathize

Practice A   Write each spelling word under the Greek root it contains.

1. *phon* means sound   _____   _____

    _____   _____

    Challenge words: _____   _____

2. *demo* means people   _____   _____

    _____   _____

3. *derm* means skin   _____   _____

    _____

4. *historia* means learning or knowing   _____

    _____   _____

5. *kardia* (or *cardia*) means heart _____   _____

Practice B   Write the spelling word next to its definition. Use a dictionary if you are not sure about the meaning of a word.

6. the study of skin _____

7. one who studies history _____

8. having to do with the heart _____

9. words that sound alike _____

10. feeling of sadness _____

11. before written history _____

12. the study of the heart _____

13. information about a population _____

14. where people study _____

15. carries sound across distance _____

Challenge words:

16. to feel sorry for _____

17. unpleasant, jarring sound _____

Name _____ **Date** _____

Subjects and Predicates

Focus

A sentence expresses a complete thought. The first word in a sentence is always capitalized, and the sentence has end punctuation. Every sentence has two parts—a **subject** and a **predicate.**

Rules

- The **simple subject** names who or what *does* or *is* something in a sentence. The simple subject and any words that describe it are called the **complete subject.**

    Example: *Elena* cleaned her room.

- The **simple predicate** of a sentence tells what the subject *does* or *is*. The simple predicate, or verb, and any words that describe it, are called the **complete predicate.**

    Example: We *went swimming in the lake.*

Practice

Read this paragraph. Circle the complete subject in each sentence. Underline the complete predicate in each sentence.

California has several interesting places to visit. Death Valley is a desert. The Death Valley region is home to many wildflowers and animals. San Diego has one of the world's largest zoos. Sacramento is the capital of California.

Name _____ Date _____

Complete and Incomplete Sentences

Focus

A **complete sentence** must have a subject and a predicate. A complete sentence expresses a complete thought.

Example: Harry's new puppy didn't eat her food.

An **incomplete sentence** is usually missing either a subject or a predicate.

Examples: Harry's new puppy. Didn't eat her food.

Practice

The following incomplete sentences are missing either a subject or predicate. Rewrite each incomplete sentence as a complete sentence.

1. Everyone in the whole town. _____

_____

2. Took the cookie away from her. _____

_____

3. The angry baseball player. _____

4. Sat on his bed for a long time. _____

_____

5. Asked his brother for a favor. _____

_____

6. The funny clown. _____

Grammar, Usage, and Mechanics • *Skills Practice 1*

Name _____ Date _____

Latin Roots

Many **Latin roots** can be found in the English language. Recognizing and knowing Latin roots can help you discover word meanings. The Latin root *form* means "shape."

Use the vocabulary words to practice identifying Latin roots.

- **platform:** a raised surface
- **uniform:** having the same form as others
- **transform:** to change in appearance
- **reform:** to make or change for the better
- **inform:** to tell

Practice **Circle the root in each word.**

1. platform

2. uniform

3. transform

4. reform

5. inform

Use each word in a sentence.

6. platform: _____

7. uniform: _____

8. transform: _____

9. reform: _____

10. inform: _____

Apply These words also have Latin roots. Use a dictionary to write the meaning of each word.

11. sensation _____

_____

12. sense _____

_____

13. sensitive _____

_____

14. sensible _____

_____

15. sensory _____

_____

16. vacant _____

_____

17. vacation _____

_____

18. vacuum _____

_____

19. evacuate _____

_____

20. vacate _____

_____

Selection Vocabulary

Focus

energy (e'•nûr•jē) *n.* the power to do work (page 154)

transferred (trants•fûrd') *v.* past tense of **transfer:** to pass along (page 155)

soar (sor) *v.* to fly high (page 155)

release (ri•lēs') *v.* to let loose (page 156)

fuels (fū'•əlz) *n.* plural form of **fuel:** something that gives energy as it is burned (page 156)

stored (stord) *adj.* having been put away for future use (page 156)

eventually (i•vent'•shə•wə•lē) *adv.* sooner or later (page 158)

contains (ken•tānz') *v.* present tense of **contain:** to hold (page 157)

Practice Circle the correct word that completes each sentence.

1. The baby eagle quickly learned to _____.

   a. release   **b.** soar   **c.** stored

2. Riley decided to _____ her pet turtle into the wild.

   a. contains   **b.** stored   **c.** release

3. I do not have enough _____ to run two miles tonight.

   a. energy   **b.** contains   **c.** transferred

4. If you don't water those plants, they will _____ die.

   a. eventually   **b.** soar   **c.** stored

5. Many _____ are found naturally under the ground.

   a. energy   **b.** stored   **c.** fuels

Apply Match each word on the left to its definition on the right.

6. eventually

a. the capacity or ability to work

7. fuels

b. carries

8. stored

c. in due time

9. contains

d. saved to be used later

10. energy

e. to let go

11. transferred

f. things that are burned for energy

12. soar

g. to glide high without much movement

13. release

h. moved from one thing to another

Name _____   Date _____

Main Idea and Details

Focus

The **main idea** is what a paragraph is about. Often, a writer provides a clear topic sentence at the beginning of a paragraph.

- The **main idea** is the most important point the writer makes in a paragraph. The main idea tells what the whole paragraph is about.

- **Details** are bits of information in the sentences of paragraphs that support the main idea.

Practice A

Find two paragraphs in "Energy Makes Things Happen" that have a clearly stated main idea. Write the page number, main idea, and two details from each paragraph.

1. Page: _____ Main Idea: _____

_____

Detail: _____

_____

Detail: _____

_____

2. Page: _____ Main Idea: _____

_____

Detail: _____

_____

Detail: _____

_____

Practice B

Read the paragraph. Underline the main idea. In the spaces, write two sentences with details that support the main idea.

Casey decided that he wanted to know more about birds. First he got some bird books from the library. Then he made a feeder from a plastic bottle and a hanger. He hung the feeder near the patio in the backyard. When he was done, Casey found a comfortable spot where he could sit and watch the woodpeckers, finches, and other birds that came for food and water.

Detail: _____

_____

Detail: _____

_____

Apply

Write a paragraph about using energy. State your main idea in the first sentence. Add sentences with details that support the main idea.

_____

_____

_____

_____

_____

_____

_____

_____

Name _____ Date _____

Summarizing and Organizing Information

Summarizing will help you organize information and remember what you have read. When you write a summary, look for the main ideas and important details, and use your own words to tell what happens in the story. Select a story from Unit 2. Write the title on the line below. Summarize the story by filling in the flow chart. Write the main ideas and important details from the story in your own words.

Title: _____

How does the story begin?
_____
_____

↓

What happens next?
_____
_____

↓

What happens after that?
_____
_____

↓

How does the story end?
_____
_____

Summarizing and Organizing Information

Choose a well-known book or movie, but do not put the title of it on the flow chart. Summarize the story on the flow chart. Then, exchange papers with a partner. Guess the title of the book or movie on your partner's flow chart. Write it on the line below.

How does the story begin?

_____

_____

↓

What happens next?

_____

_____

↓

What happens after that?

_____

_____

↓

How does the story end?

_____

_____

Can you guess the title? Write it here.

_____

Title guessed by (name): _____

Inquiry • *Skills Practice 1*

Latin Roots

Focus Many English words contain **Latin roots.** If you know the spellings and meanings of common Latin roots, you can figure out how to spell and define words that contain them.

- The Latin root *dict* means say or speak.
- The Latin root *scribe* means write.
- The Latin roots *port* and *fer* mean carry.
- The Latin root *creat* means to make new.

Practice A **Write each spelling word under the Latin root it contains.**

1. dict means say or speak

_____   _____

_____   _____

Challenge words:

_____   _____

2. scribe means write

_____   _____

_____   _____

3. port means carry

_____   _____

_____   _____

4. fer means carry

_____   _____

_____   _____

5. creat means to make new

_____   _____

_____   _____

Practice B

Match each spelling word with its definition. Use a dictionary if you are not sure about the meaning of a word.

_____ **6.** creature

_____ **7.** subscribe

_____ **8.** contradict

_____ **9.** export

_____ **10.** creative

_____ **11.** referral

_____ **12.** transcribe

_____ **13.** diction

_____ **14.** report

_____ **15.** defer

_____ **16.** predict

_____ **17.** support

_____ **18.** infer

A. someone who has been sent

B. to provide assistance

C. to copy

D. a living creation

E. likely to have new ideas

F. to say before

G. to sign a promise to pay

H. clarity of pronunciation

I. sell outside the country

J. to say the opposite

K. to give information

L. to put off

M. to conclude

Apply

Use each of the challenge words to write a sentence.

19. dictator _____

20. dictionary _____

Name _____ Date _____

Using Quotation Marks

Focus Use **quotation marks**

Rule	Example
• to set off the exact words of a speaker in dialogue or direct speech	• "Yeah," Leanne answered, "it's going to be a great party!"
• around a direct quote from another work or text	• Renaldo "knew Jinx was excited" when he told her about his idea.
• around the title of a poem or a short story	• "Hippopotamus" by Barbara Juster Esbensen
• If the speaker's words form a question, place the question mark *inside* the quotation marks. If the quotation does not form a question, the question mark is placed *outside* the quotation marks.	• "What time are you leaving to go to the party?" Leanne asked. Why does the invitation say, "Do not wear jeans"?

Practice Read this dialogue. Put quotation marks where needed.

Dominic and Kendra, please come here, Mom said. Have you taken

Freckles out for her walk yet?

I did it last time, Dominic complained. It's Kendra's turn!

Says who? said Kendra. I always take Freckles on her walks!

Please stop arguing, Mom said. Why don't both of you walk Freckles?

Apply Read the following sentences carefully. If the quotation marks have been used correctly in the sentence, write *C*. If the quotation marks have been used incorrectly, write *I*. Then write the sentence correctly on the lines provided.

1. "A Gingered January" is my favorite poem in the book.

_____

2. The poem "I Met a Rat of Culture has a lot of interesting words in it."

_____

_____

3. "What movie do you want to see?" asked Jeanne.

_____

4. "I'd like to watch a musical," Lucy answered.

_____

5. I wrote a poem "called My Sweet Caroline."

_____

6. "February Hero" and April Medicine are two poems in a book by Joyce Carol Thomas.

_____

_____

7. "Why don't you join us"? asked Mother.

_____

_____

8. "Well," said Jack, "it's about time you read that book!"

_____

Name _____ **Date** _____

Synonyms

Synonyms are words that have similar meanings. Read the following definitions and use these words to complete the exercise below.

mural: a picture painted on a wall or ceiling

restoring: putting or bringing back together

riot: a disturbance of the public peace by three or more persons

confident: having trust or faith

occupation: the work a person does in order to earn a living

Complete each set of synonyms with one vocabulary word.

1. repairing, mending, fixing, _____

2. job, business, employment, _____

3. painting, photograph, scene, _____

4. confusion, commotion, disorder, _____

5. positive, certain, assured, _____

Analogy

An **analogy** is the relationship between two pairs of words.

- **Call** is to **shout** as **high** is to **tall.**

This is a **synonym analogy.** The words **call** and **shout** are related to each other because they mean almost the same thing. The words **high** and **tall** are related to each other because they also mean almost the same thing.

Complete the following analogies with one of the words in the parentheses.

6. **Close** is to **shut** as **glare** is to _____.
   (answer, flash, talk)

7. **Divide** is to **separate** as **daring** is to _____.
   (timid, cold, bold)

8. **Go** is to **leave** as **clarify** is to _____.
   (talk, explain, read)

9. **City** is to **town** as **despair** is to _____.
   (happy, gloom, nice)

10. **Great** is to **large** as **narrate** is to _____.
    (describe, walk, run)

11. **Keep** is to **hold** as **nightmare** is to _____.
    (bad dream, sleep, wake)

12. **Right** is to **correct** as **prepare** is to _____.
    (arrange, account, move)

13. **Pain** is to **hurt** as **scare** is to _____.
    (unafraid, terror, happy)

14. **Late** is to **tardy** as **earned** is to _____.
    (deserved, took, fair)

Name _____ Date _____

Selection Vocabulary

Focus

linked (linkt) *v.* past tense of **link:** to connect (page 172)

slightly (slīt•lē) *adv.* by a little bit (page 173)

depend (di•pend') *v.* to need; to rely (page 176)

microscope (mī•krə•skōp') *n.* a tool for looking at very small things (page 179)

bitterly (bi'•tûr•lē) *adv.* harshly; extremely (page 180)

seaweed (sē•wēd) *n.* a plant that grows near the surface of the sea (page 182)

branch (branch) *v.* to divide and subdivide (page 184)

Practice Write the vocabulary word next to the group of words that have a similar meaning.

1. harshly; extremely; severely _____

2. telescope; magnifying glass; lens _____

3. trust; rely; need _____

4. attached; connected; joined _____

5. barely; hardly; by a little bit _____

6. divide; spread; offshoot _____

7. kelp; algae; rockweed _____

Apply Fill in each blank with a vocabulary word from this lesson to complete each sentence.

8. _____ is actually quite delicious.

9. Philip needed a _____ to study the tiny cells.

10. The two girls _____ their arms together and began to skip.

11. The freezing rain slapped him _____ in the face.

12. As babies get older, they _____ less on their parents.

13. If we _____ off in different directions, we have a better chance of finding our puppy.

14. He tapped the cone _____ with his car and it didn't fall.

Name _____ Date _____

Making Inferences

Readers **make inferences** about characters and events to understand a total picture in a story.

An **inference** is a statement a reader makes about a character or event from the story. To make an inference, the reader uses

- **information** from the story, such as examples, facts, reasons, and descriptions.

- **personal experience or knowledge,** such as memories and experiences the reader brings to the story.

Practice A Think of an event from "Who Eats What?" Write an inference about the event, such as why you think it happens or happened. Write the information from the story and the personal experience you used to make the inference.

Event: _____

_____

Inference: _____

_____

Information from the story: _____

_____

_____

Personal experience: _____

_____

_____

Practice B — Read the following paragraph. Then make an inference by answering the questions.

Harry's father and mother would be angry when they saw the table even though Harry had not meant to break it. He accidentally fell on the table while tossing a football in the house. Harry looked at the broken pieces scattered around the room. He knew the table could not be fixed.

1. What did Harry do? _____

_____

2. Is Harry worried? Why? _____

_____

3. Can Harry fix the table? Why? _____

_____

Apply — Write a paragraph that continues the above story about Harry and the table. Include the inferences you made and add information that will let your readers make new inferences.

_____

_____

_____

_____

_____

_____

Name _____ Date _____

Resource List

It is important to use several different sources to research your ideas, so you can cross-check information, or make sure it is correct. Different sources can also give you different types of information. This will provide you with a broader picture of your topic.

Look over the list of resources, and place a checkmark by each resource you have used or plan to use when researching your topic.

☐ encyclopedias   ☐ magazines and newspapers

☐ atlas   ☐ the Internet

☐ books

Answer the following questions about resources.

1. Which resource would give you the most recent information on a topic?

_____

2. Where is the best place to look for maps to aid your research?

_____

3. Some resources are less reliable than others. Which resource should you be most cautious about when using it for research?

_____

_____

4. Why might this resource be less than reliable at times?

_____

_____

5. If you want some basic, general information on a broad topic, where might you look?

_____

Resource List

People and places are other resources that can be very helpful to you as you conduct your research. Interviewing people and visiting places can bring a unique perspective to your topic.

1. Who will you interview about your topic?

_____

_____

2. What questions will you ask this person?

_____

_____

_____

3. What are some places you could visit to help you research your topic?

_____

_____

4. Choose a place to visit. What will you do while you're there?

_____

_____

5. Think of a creative way to use what you've learned from people and places in your research presentation. What might you do to enhance your project?

_____

_____

_____

Inquiry • *Skills Practice 1*

Name _____ Date _____

Informative Reports

Think | **Audience: Who** will read your informative report?

_____

Purpose: What is your reason for writing an informative report?

_____

Prewriting | Use the time line to organize the information you gathered about the invention in sequential order. Use a separate sheet of paper to add more boxes, if necessary.

Event:

Date:

Revising   Use this checklist to revise your description.

☐ Have you presented facts and examples objectively?

☐ Have you located information in multiple sources?

☐ Did you organize the information in sequential order?

☐ Did you define any terms that may be unfamiliar to your readers?

☐ Did you include ideas about how the invention affects your life?

Editing/Proofreading   Use this checklist to correct mistakes in your revised draft.

☐ Did you double-check the facts you used?

☐ Did you check your spellings, especially names and titles?

☐ If you used a direct quote, did you use quotation marks correctly?

Publishing   Use this checklist to prepare your research report for publication.

☐ Write or type a final copy. Include a bibliography.

☐ Include a diagram, an illustration, or a photograph.

Name _____   Date _____

Synonyms

Focus Synonyms are words that have similar meanings.

Practice A **Write the spelling words that belong with each phrase below.**

1. almost the same

_____ _____

2. place to live

_____ _____

_____

3. bang together

_____ _____

4. break apart

_____ _____

_____

5. looked or watched

_____ _____

_____

6. people who work together

_____ _____

Word List

1. spotted
2. spied
3. viewed
4. slightly
5. somewhat
6. branch
7. divide
8. split
9. alike
10. similar
11. home
12. dwelling
13. residence
14. partner
15. teammate
16. crash
17. collide
18. cheerful
19. happy
20. merry

Challenge Words:

21. enormous
22. gigantic
23. massive

Practice B

Write the spelling word that you think has the best meaning to complete each sentence. Use a dictionary if you need to check on definitions.

7. My _____ (partner, teammate) hit a homerun.

8. We can _____ (branch, split) the money we earned.

9. Fresh flowers made the room more _____ (cheerful, merry).

10. No two snowflakes are exactly _____ (alike, similar)

11. The governor's _____ (dwelling, residence) is near the capitol.

12. He _____ (spotted, viewed) the eclipse cautiously.

13. I ate _____ (slightly, somewhat) more ice cream than you did.

14. Mr. Shepherd's business will soon _____ (branch, divide) out.

15. Can you hear the waves _____ (crash, collide) on the beach?

Apply

Fill in the missing letters to write the whole spelling word.

16. sp   d   _____

17. som   w   t   _____

18.   elling   _____

Challenge

19.   nor   s   _____

20. gigan   _____

Name _____ Date _____

Compound Subjects

Focus

A **compound subject** is two or more subjects that have the same predicate in a sentence.

Example: **John and Erica** live in two different cities.

The verb in the sentence must agree in number with the subject in a sentence.

Example: Joe **lives** in Maine. Joe and Aly **live** in Maine.

| Frodo and Popper | Mike and Gabe |
| Our computer and our television | California and Oregon |

Practice A Fill in the blanks with a compound subject from the box above.

1. _____ decided to join the Boy Scouts.

2. _____ are my two new puppies.

3. _____ have beautiful landscapes.

4. _____ need to be replaced.

Practice B Fill in the blanks with a compound subject of your choice.

5. _____ ate their ice cream faster than everyone else.

6. _____ are my two favorite colors.

Apply

Circle all the compound subjects in the following paragraph.

California is a state with a lot to offer. Almonds, dates, and olives

are grown there. Movies and TV shows are made there as well.

Children and adults enjoy skiing in the mountains. They also like

to swim in the ocean. Both tourists and locals can find plenty to

do and see in California.

**Write a sentence for each pair of bold-faced words, using
the two words as a compound subject.**

7. **Katie, teacher** _____

_____

8. **boy, dog** _____

_____

9. **carrots, potatoes** _____

_____

10. **table, chairs** _____

_____

11. **Lyle, Kyle** _____

_____

12. **January, February** _____

_____

_____

Grammar, Usage, and Mechanics • *Skills Practice 1*

Name _____ Date _____

Antonyms

Antonyms are words that mean the opposite or almost the opposite of other words.

good and **bad**

tall and **short**

After reading the passage, write one antonym for each underlined word.

About fifty percent of Americans are overweight. An overweight person can lose weight by doing <u>proper</u> exercises, like walking, and eating healthful foods, like fruits and vegetables. Every person, <u>young</u> and old, should exercise and eat healthful foods, even if they don't want to lose weight. Whether or not you want to lose weight, it's a good idea to keep exercising so your muscles stay <u>firm</u>. Remember, it's okay to want to be <u>slender</u>, but not every person is built to be the same size. Weight loss is not a <u>rapid</u> process, so do not expect to lose a lot of weight in a short period of time.

1. proper _____

2. young _____

3. firm _____

4. slender _____

5. rapid _____

Analogy

Focus

An **analogy** is two pairs of words that are related in the same way.

- **Front** is to **back** as **left** is to **right**.

Front is the opposite of *back* and *left* is the opposite of *right*. This is an **antonym analogy**.

- **Happy** is to **sad** as **hurry** is to **slow**.
- **Hot** is to **cold** as **full** is to **empty**.

Practice   Complete the antonym analogies with a word from inside the parentheses.

6. **Lost** is to **found** as **outside** is to _____.
   (indoors, inside, home)

7. **Keep** is to **give** as **enjoyment** is to _____.
   (displeasure, hate, unlike)

8. **Bad** is to **good** as **destroy** is to _____.
   (create, nice, form)

9. **Noisy** is to **quiet** as **appoint** is to _____.
   (dismiss, stop, pause)

10. **Positive** is to **negative** as **ground** is to _____.
    (sky, flower, rain)

Apply   Use these words to create antonym analogies.

11. rapid _____

12. firm _____

13. proper _____

14. young _____

15. slender _____

Name _____ Date _____

Selection Vocabulary

Focus

shrivel (shri'•vəl) *v.* to wrinkle and become small (page 194)

droop (dro͞op) *v.* to sink; to hang down (page 195)

brittle (bri'•təl) *adj.* easily broken (page 195)

decays (di•kāz) *v.* present tense of **decay:** to slowly break down (page 195)

swarming (swor'•ming) *v.* form of **swarm:** to gather or live in a large group (page 196)

burrow (bûr•ō) *n.* a hole in the ground to live in (page 197)

circulate (sûr'•kyə•lāt) *v.* to flow around freely (page 200)

predator (pre'•də•tûr) *n.* any animal that lives by hunting another animal for food (page 201)

Practice

Write the word from the word box that matches each definition below.

1. _____ to distribute in a wide area

2. _____ slowly diminishes or rots

3. _____ gathering in a horde

4. _____ an animal that kills and eats other animals

5. _____ to shrink and become wrinkled

6. _____ very fragile

7. _____ to bend downward

8. _____ a house for an animal dug underground

Apply Circle the word in parentheses that best fits each sentence.

9. The bees were (swarming/shrivel) around a single flower.

10. What happens to a pumpkin after it (burrow/decays)?

11. Trent opened the windows so air could (burrow/circulate) through the house.

12. When my cat tries to catch a bird, she is a (predator/droop).

13. When grapes (shrivel/decays), they become raisins.

14. My flowers need water. They're starting to (swarming/droop).

15. Be careful when you mount that butterfly. Its wings are very (brittle/circulate).

16. The mole hid in its (burrow/predator).

Name _____ Date _____

Fact and Opinion

Focus

Writers use **facts and opinions** to support ideas in their writing.

- A **fact** is a statement than can be proven true.
- An **opinion** is what someone feels or believes is true. Opinions cannot be proven true or false.

Practice A

Look through "What Rot! Nature's Mighty Recycler" for examples of facts and opinions. Write two facts and two opinions on the lines below.

1. Page: _____

Opinion: _____

_____

2. Page: _____

Fact: _____

_____

3. Page: _____

Opinion: _____

_____

4. Page: _____

Fact: _____

_____

Practice B   Read the sentences below. Write *fact* if the
sentence is a fact or *opinion* if it is an opinion
in the spaces below.

5. _____ All German shepherd dogs are mammals.

6. _____ The success of a business depends on the age
of its owners.

7. _____ Chicago is a city in the state of Illinois.

8. _____ The *Titanic* was a large ship that sank in the
Atlantic Ocean.

9. _____ Being on salary is better than taking a
percentage of the income.

Apply   Write two sentences that are facts and two
sentences that are opinions about the town
or city in which you live.

10. _____

_____

11. _____

_____

12. _____

_____

13. _____

_____

Comprehension Skill • *Skills Practice 1*

Name _____ Date _____

Diagrams

A diagram is an illustration of the parts of an object, an arrangement of objects, the steps in a process, or the stages in a cycle. Diagrams clarify written information in a book, magazine, or other resource by providing a picture to help readers see how things work.

Here are the kinds of information diagrams can show:

- They can show how something is put together, such as roller skates.

- They can show how something is arranged, such as furniture in a room.

- Diagrams can also show how something works, such as the hip or elbow joints in the body.

- They can show how to make something, such as a model airplane.

- Diagrams can show what steps make up a process, such as making steel.

- They can also show what stages make up a cycle, such as the life cycle of a frog.

Look at the diagram below.

Parts of an In-Line Skate

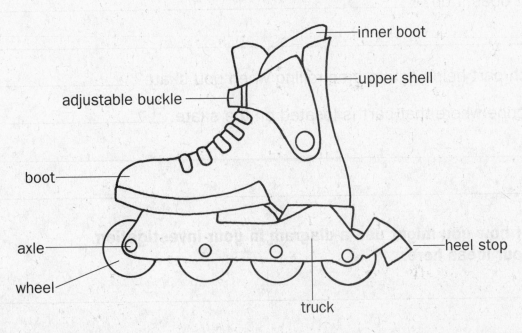

Diagrams

Notice the features of the diagram on page 109. These features are common to most diagrams.

- The **title** of a diagram tells what the diagram shows.
- **Labels** of a diagram tell about the parts of an object or the steps in a process.
- **Lines** lead from each label to a part of an object or one step in a process.
- **Arrows** show the order in which the steps of a process or the stages in a cycle take place. They may also show movement or direction.

Answer the following questions using the diagram of an in-line skate.

1. What parts of an in-line skate cover the foot and part of the leg?

_____

_____

2. Can you tell what the truck does by looking at the diagram? _____

What does it do? _____

_____

3. Which part helps you to stop rolling when you skate? _____

Describe where that part is located on the skate. _____

_____

_____

Think of how you might use a diagram in your investigation. Write your ideas here.

_____

_____

Name _____ Date _____

Antonyms

Focus

- **Antonyms** are words that have opposite, or almost opposite, meanings.
- An analogy is two pairs of words that are related in the same way.

  Example: night is to day as up is to down.

Practice A Write the spelling word that completes each analogy below.

1. **Over** is to **under** as **inside** is to _____.

2. **Loud** is to **quiet** as **noisy** is to _____.

3. **Hero** is to **villain** as **friend** is to _____.

4. **Bird** is to **insect** as
   predator is to _____.

5. **Joyful** is to **sad** as **proud** is to _____.

6. **Rude** is to **polite** as **insult** is to _____.

7. **Up** is to **down** as **positive** is to _____.

Challenge

8. **Rough** is to **smooth** as
   brittle is to _____.

Word List

1. insult
2. compliment
3. silent
4. noisy
5. proud
6. ashamed
7. positive
8. negative
9. friend
10. enemy
11. predator
12. prey
13. build
14. destroy
15. divide
16. unite
17. inside
18. outside
19. comedy
20. tragedy

Challenge Words

21. brittle
22. flexible

Practice B
Look up these spelling words and write a short definition for each one.

9. insult _____

10. noisy _____

11. predator _____

12. unite _____

13. destroy _____

14. tragedy _____

Challenge

15. brittle _____

Apply
Circle the misspelled word in each sentence and write the correct spelling on the line provided.

16. Roman wants to bild a treehouse. _____

17. My freind, Abby, has a pet spider. _____

18. Mother was positve she was right. _____

19. Tigers pray on wild boars. _____

20. I was prowd of my blue ribbon. _____

Name _____ Date _____

Compound Predicates

A **compound predicate** is two or more predicates that have the same subject in a sentence.

Example: The dog **walked** around the room and **sniffed** the furniture.

Some of the following sentences have a compound predicate, and some do not. Put an *X* by each sentence that has a compound predicate.

1. Nicki and Zach ate lunch together. _____

2. Shawna finished her breakfast and got dressed for school. _____

3. Terrell peeked around the corner at Carla. _____

4. Lainey and I walked the dog and gave him a bone. _____

5. Hattie broke her arm and went to the hospital. _____

6. My parakeet chirps all night and sleeps all day. _____

7. We played on the playground after lunch. _____

8. My mom jumped up and down and kissed my dad. _____

Apply   Add your own words at the end of each sentence to turn the simple predicate into a compound predicate. The first one has been done for you.

9. My mom baked a cake <u>and took it to our neighbor.</u>

10. Lisa called Mary on the phone _____

_____

11. My cat played with her yarn _____

_____

12. The doctor checked my throat _____

_____

13. My dad fell asleep in his chair _____

_____

14. I emptied the trash _____

_____

Read this paragraph. Circle the complete subject in each sentence. Underline the complete predicate in each sentence. Write CS above any compound subjects and CP above any compound predicates.

David began to take tennis lessons. He learned how to hit

the ball and how to hold his racket. David and his brother

practiced for many hours each day. His coach told David that

he was ready for his first tennis tournament. David played

hard and served the ball well. He won the tournament.

Name _____ Date _____

Homographs

Focus

Homographs are words that are spelled the same but have different pronunciations and meanings.

Vocabulary words

- **present:** not absent
- **sole:** type of fish
- **object:** a thing
- **entrance:** delight; charm

Practice Write another meaning for these words.

1. present _____

2. sole _____

3. object _____

4. entrance _____

Apply The words in the sentences are underlined because they have different pronunciations and meanings. Write the meaning of each underlined word in the sentences. You should have two different meanings for each sentence.

Example: I will **present** her with a **present** at the party.

   present—to give   *present*—a gift.

The doctor <u>wound</u> a bandage around her <u>wound</u>.

5. _____   6. _____

I will <u>lead</u> you through a tour of the <u>lead</u> mine.

7. _____   8. _____

Did you <u>record</u> her <u>record</u> breaking jump?

9. _____   10. _____

The fishermen had a <u>row</u> as they sat in a <u>row</u> on their fishing boat.

11. _____   12. _____

The <u>dove</u> <u>dove</u> off the branch and flew to the ground.

13. _____   14. _____

There was a <u>minute</u> change in the experiment after watching it for a <u>minute</u>.

15. _____   16. _____

The girl with the <u>bow</u> in her hair stood on the <u>bow</u> of the ship.

17. _____   18. _____

Name _____ Date _____

Selection Vocabulary

Focus

ancestors (an'•ses'•tûrz) *n.* plural of noun **ancestor:** someone from long ago who is a direct relation to you, for example a great-great-grandparent (page 210)

pollinate (po'•lə•nāt) *v.* to spread pollen from flower to flower, allowing fruit and seeds to grow (page 212)

wither (wi'•thûr) *v.* to dry up, to shrivel (page 212)

smoldering (smōl•dûr•ing) *adj.* burning and smoking without flames (page 212)

oxygen (ok'•si•jən) *n.* a gas that makes up about one-fifth of Earth's atmosphere and that animals must breathe to live (page 214)

clinging (kling'•ing) *v.* form of **cling:** to hold on tight (page 216)

start (stärt) *n.* a jump due to a surprise (page 218)

dangle (dang'•gəl) *v.* to hang; to swing loosely (page 220)

Practice

Write *T* in the blank if the sentence for the vocabulary word is correct. Write *F* if the sentence is false. For each *F* answer, write the word that fits the definition.

1. If something is *smoldering,* it is holding on tight. ____ _____

2. If you have a *dangle,* you jump from surprise. ____ _____

3. Animals must breathe *oxygen* to live. ____ _____

4. *Pollinate* means "spread pollen from flower to flower." ____ _____

5. Your great-grandparents are your *ancestors.* ____ _____

6. If something is *clinging,* it is burning or smoking without flames.

____ _____

7. *Dangle* means "to dry up and shrivel." ____ _____

Apply   Write the word that best fits each clue below.

8. We must breathe this to live. What is it?

_____

9. These people are relatives of yours who lived long ago.

Who are they? _____

10. The baby monkey was hanging on to its mother tightly.

What was he doing? _____

11. When bees do this to flowers, it helps fruit and seeds to grow.

What is it? _____

12. If your front baby teeth hang by a thread before you pull them out,

what do they do? _____

13. You do this when someone scares you. What is it?

_____

14. A forest is doing this when there is smoke without flames.

What is it? _____

15. When flowers dry up, we say they do this. What is it?

_____

Name _____   Date _____

Classify and Categorize

Focus Good readers classify items into categories as they read to help them organize information and understand what they read.

Classifying means arranging people, animals, or things into different groups or **categories.** When classifying people, ideas, places, or things

- name the categories, or groups, for similar items.

- list items that fit the category.

Animals ⟵—— *Category*
Bats
Lizards
Mice
Fish
Turtles

Some items can fit more than one category.

Animals	**Reptiles**
Turtles	Turtles
Lizards	Lizards

Practice **Look through "The Great Kapok Tree" and list all the items that fit the categories below.**

1. Rainforest animals: _____

_____

2. Birds: _____

_____

3. Mammals: _____

_____

Apply

Look at the items in the box below. List each item from the box under the correct category. Remember that some items can fit into more than one category.

Items

notebook	fruit	juice	sandwich
stamps	paper	pen	

Things for Lunch   **School Supplies**   **Things for Writing and Mailing Letters**

_____   _____   _____

_____   _____   _____

_____   _____   _____

Whales have characteristics that make them different from other types of sea creatures. For instance, whales are mammals. Think of other types of animals, such as reptiles or birds. Name and write this new category for a type of animal. Then, list any animals that fit this category in the spaces below.

_____

_____

_____

_____

_____

_____

Name _____   Date _____

Using Visual Aids

Charts, graphs and tables are visual presentations of information. Use them to present a lot of information in a small amount of space.

- There are many types of charts, tables and graphs. The following is an example of a **chart.** Charts contain rows and columns. Each row and column tells what type of information is in the chart.

Which foods do the birds like best?

	Suet	Millet	Peanut Hearts	Thistle	Cracked Corn
Blue Jay	x		x		
Finch	x			x	
Grosbeak	x				
Dove	x	x	x		x

- A **pie chart** is a circle that breaks things down into parts of a whole.

- A **bar graph** compares things or shows how something has changed.

What's in that Birdbrain Deluxe birdfood mixture?

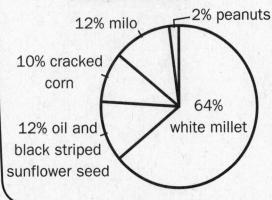

12% milo
2% peanuts
10% cracked corn
64% white millet
12% oil and black striped sunflower seed

Percentage of Schools with Internet Access

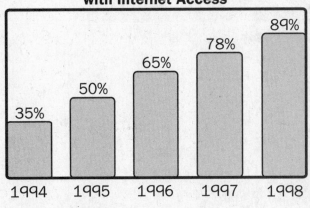

35% 1994 50% 1995 65% 1996 78% 1997 89% 1998

Use the birdfeeding chart to answer these questions.

1. Which birds like to eat millet? _____

2. What do finches like to eat? _____

3. What food do all the birds eat? _____

Using Visual Aids

Read the paragraph below. Turn the information into a chart or graph and give it a title.

This is information about major earthquakes in the United States in the 20th century. There was an earthquake in San Francisco, California, on April 18, 1906. It measured 7.7 on the Richter scale and caused 700 deaths. An earthquake in Prince William Sound, Alaska, on March 27, 1964, measured 9.2 on the Richter scale and caused 130 deaths. An earthquake in Yucca Valley, California, on June 28, 1992, measured 7.6 and caused one death.

Name _____ Date _____

Writing a Persuasive Report

Audience: Who will read your persuasive report?

_____

Purpose: What do you want your readers to think about your report?

_____

Prewriting

Use this graphic organizer to plan your persuasive report. Write your opinion in the middle circle. Then write your supporting facts on the lines. Think about how you want to present your facts. You might choose to start with your strongest point or build up to it and state it last.

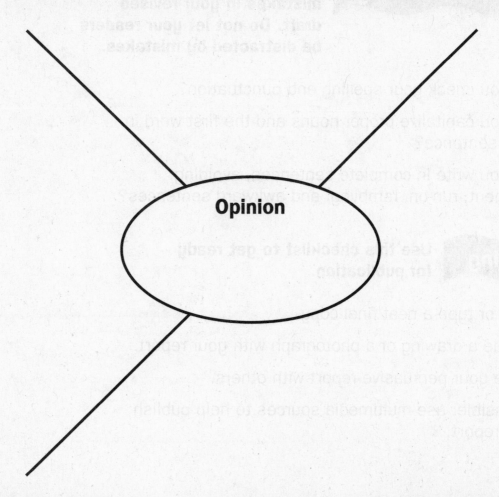

Opinion

Revising

Use this checklist to revise your description.

☐ Has the purpose you chose during prewriting been met?

☐ Did you clearly state your opinion?

☐ Did you include facts that support your opinion?

☐ Did you begin in a way that will grab your audience's attention?

☐ Will readers be able to tell that the topic is important to you?

☐ Did you organize your facts in a logical order?

Editing/Proofreading

Use this checklist to correct mistakes in your revised draft. Do not let your readers be distracted by mistakes.

☐ Did you check your spelling and punctuation?

☐ Did you capitalize proper nouns and the first word in each sentence?

☐ Did you write in complete sentences, avoiding fragment, run-on, rambling, and awkward sentences?

Publishing

Use this checklist to get ready for publication.

☐ Write or type a neat final copy.

☐ Include a drawing or a photograph with your report.

☐ Share your persuasive report with others.

☐ If possible, use multimedia sources to help publish your report.

Name _____ Date _____

Homographs

Focus **Homographs** are words that are spelled the same way, but they have different meanings and origins. Homographs may also be pronounced differently.

Practice A Read each sentence below. Underline spelling words that are used as nouns. Circle those used as verbs. Draw a box around spelling words that are used as adjectives.

1. Local farmers produce and sell fresh produce at the market.

2. My coach will contest the referee's call if it's a close contest.

3. A hawk dove to close in on the dove.

4. There was a defect in the soldier's plan to defect.

5. There is no excuse for failing to say, "Please excuse me."

6. A minute ago, the nurse wound the bandage around the wound.

7. I object when a minute object is thrown at me.

8. Dad upset me by shouting about the upset in the championship game.

Word List

1. record
2. project
3. produce
4. minute
5. resent
6. wound
7. excuse
8. contest
9. close
10. present
11. object
12. extract
13. compress
14. resort
15. console
16. address
17. perfect
18. dove
19. upset
20. defect

Challenge Words

21. separate
22. document

Practice B

Look at the pronunciation for each of these spelling words. Use the word to write a definition. You may use a dictionary to check the meaning.

9. pro' jekt _____

10. ri zent' _____

11. pres' ənt _____

12. kom' pres _____

13. per fekt' _____

Challenge

14. sep' e rate _____

Apply

Circle the misspelled words in this paragraph. Write the words correctly on the lines provided.

The spy put the dockument beside the stolen objict on the consoll. He did not rezort to hurting the people at the adress he had been given, but he knew they were upset. His partner was prezent, but not close by. He had gone into a seperate room to find a kompress for his wound.

15. _____

16. _____

17. _____

18. _____

19. _____

20. _____

21. _____

22. _____

Name _____   Date _____

Compound Sentences

Focus

A **conjunction** is a word that connects words or groups of words. The words *and, but,* and *or* are **coordinating conjunctions.** They connect related words or groups of words.

Examples: You may mow the grass **or** help me wash the car.

Alex can help you, **but** she has other chores to do too.

Combine two simple sentences by adding a conjunction to form a **compound sentence.**

Example: Sally decided to rest. She wasn't really tired.

Sally decided to rest, **but** she wasn't really tired.

Practice

Combine each of these pairs of simple sentences to form a compound sentence using a coordinating conjunction.

1. We could play tennis. We could go swimming. _____

_____

2. Vince picked up the phone. He dialed the number. _____

_____

3. My teacher fell on the ice. He broke his arm. _____

_____

4. Mr. DeCarlo will get our mail. His wife will do it. _____

_____

Apply   **Read the following draft. Then improve it by combining sentences to form compound sentences. Write your revision in the space provided.**

Jillian bought a new kite. Tarah helped her put it together. Jillian tried it first. Tarah watched. Jillian said Tarah could try it. She wouldn't force her. Tarah decided to try it. She was successful. The kite flew high in the sky. The girls were excited. Their smiles soon turned to frowns. The kite was caught in a tree. Jillian went to get her dad. He got a ladder. He got the kite out of the tree.

_____

_____

_____

_____

_____

_____

_____

_____

_____

_____

Name _____ Date _____

Greek Roots

Focus

Many English words come from Greek. If you know the spellings and meanings of common **Greek roots,** you can figure out how to spell and define words with these roots.

Example:
monarchy: **mon** means "one," and **arch** means "ruler"
biography: **bio** means "life," and **graph** means "write"
democracy: **dem** means "people"
generation: **gen** means "birth"

The Greek root **cycl** means "circle."
The Greek root **tele** means "far off."
The Greek root **logy** means "to speak."
The Greek root **port** means "to carry."

Practice A

Based on what you know about English words that come from Greek, write a definition for each of the following words.

1. telegraph _____

_____

2. bicycle _____

3. autograph _____

_____

4. biology _____

_____

Practice B | Write the word from the word box that matches each definition.

geology	paragraph	apology	geography
recycle	tricycle	technology	photograph
telegram	graphics		

5. a vehicle with three wheels _____

6. the study of rocks, mountains, and cliffs _____

7. a group of sentences about the same topic _____

8. a picture that is made by a camera _____

9. saying you are sorry _____

10. to use something over again _____

11. a message sent from far away _____

12. methods and devices used in science _____

13. the science dealing with Earth's surface _____

14. pictures and designs _____

Apply | Use two of the words from the word box in a single sentence.

_____

_____

_____

Name _____ Date _____

Selection Vocabulary

Focus

declared (di • klârd') *v.* past tense of **declare:** to announce (page 240)

independence (in' • də • pen' • dənts) *n.* freedom from the control of another country (page 240)

original (ə • rij' • ə • nəl) *adj.* first (page 240)

settle (se' • təl) *v.* to decide (page 241)

contribute (kən • tri' • byət) *v.* to give money or time (page 242)

proper (pro' • pûr) *adj.* suitable; correct (page 253)

violate (vī' • ə • lāt') *v.* to fail to obey; to break (page 254)

Practice **Fill in each blank with a vocabulary word from this lesson to complete each sentence.**

1. I don't think that is the _____ way to tie a slip knot.

2. Baby animals often gain their _____ from their parents before children do.

3. You may go hiking as long as you don't _____ any of the park's rules.

4. Isabel and Jorge need to _____ their disagreement.

5. My parents would like to _____ a sum of money to a local charity.

6. The president _____ that today will be a national holiday.

7. The Detroit Red Wings are one of the _____ six hockey teams.

Apply

Write the word from the word box that matches each definition below.

8. _____ not relying on others

9. _____ to donate something to someone

10. _____ said

11. _____ first of a kind

12. _____ to break a rule

13. _____ right or appropriate

14. _____ to resolve

Name _____ Date _____

Main Idea and Supporting Details

Focus Writers use a main idea and details to make their point clear in a paragraph.

- The **main idea** is the most important point the writer makes in a paragraph. The main idea tells what the whole paragraph is about.

- **Details** are bits of information in the sentences of paragraphs that support the main idea.

Practice A Find a paragraph in "The U.S. Constitution and You" that has a clearly stated main idea. Write the page number and main idea of the paragraph. Then, list two sentences with details the writer gives to support the main idea.

Page: _____

Main Idea: _____

_____

Detail: _____

_____

_____

Detail: _____

_____

_____

Practice B

Read the paragraph below. Underline the main idea. Then, write two sentences with details that support the main idea.

Our ears are the organs of hearing and balance. They collect sound vibrations from the air and turn them into messages called nerve signals that are sent to the brain. Each ear has three main parts: the outer ear, the middle ear, and the inner ear. The outer ear is the part you see. The middle ear consists of the eardrum and three tiny bones called the ossicles. The main part of the inner ear is the cochlea, which changes vibrations into nerve signals. The inner ear also makes sure that the body keeps its balance.

Detail: _____

_____

Detail: _____

_____

Apply

Write a paragraph about government or politics. State your main idea in the first sentence. Then, add sentences with details to support your main idea.

_____

_____

_____

_____

_____

_____

Name _____ Date _____

Using Time Lines

A **time line** can help you understand when important events occurred and the order in which they happened. A time line may cover any length of time, from the lifetime of a person to a historical period of hundreds or thousands of years.

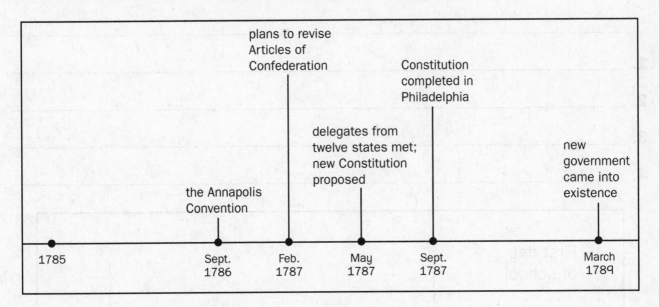

Here are some things to remember about time lines.

• Each dot on the line represents a date.

• Each dot represents at least one event.

• A time line usually has a title that indicates the type of information that is shown on the line.

• Events are listed on the time line from left to right in the order of occurrence. The earliest event appears at the far left.

• A time line can be made for any set of events. However, time lines usually show meaningful relationships between events.

• Record only important events on a time line. Avoid minor details and unimportant events.

Using Time Lines (continued)

What important school events have happened since the first day of school? Make a time line of these events from the first day of school to today. Begin by listing four important events and the dates of these events in the spaces below. Then put the dates and a brief description of each event on the time line in the box.

_____

1. _____

2. _____

3. _____

4. _____

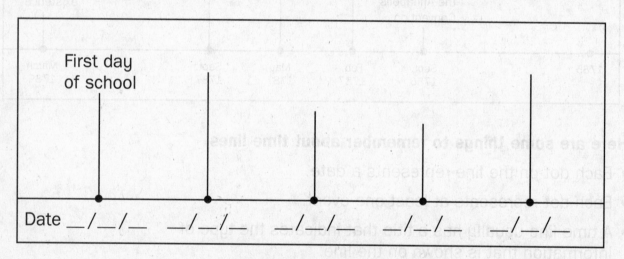

First day of school

Date __/__/__   __/__/__   __/__/__   __/__/__   __/__/__

How might you use a time line during your investigation?

_____

_____

_____

_____

Name _____ Date _____

Spelling

Focus

- **Homophones** are words that sound alike, but homophones are spelled differently and have different meanings.

Example: *choose* and *chews*

- Understanding the meanings of homophones helps you use the words correctly.

Practice | Look at each pair of homophones. Write the missing letters in each word.

1. hir_____   h_____er

2. _____ites   ri_____ts

3. p_____ce   pe_____ce

4. b_____k   br_____

5. ch_____se   ch_____

6. thro_____   th_____

7. fl_____er   fl_____r

Challenge

8. f_____s   ph_____

Word List

1. *hire*
2. *higher*
3. *through*
4. *threw*
5. *passed*
6. *past*
7. *writes*
8. *rights*
9. *frees*
10. *freeze*
11. *wood*
12. *would*
13. *piece*
14. *peace*
15. *flower*
16. *flour*
17. *chews*
18. *choose*
19. *break*
20. *brake*

Challenge Words

21. *phrase*
22. *frays*

Apply Look for homophone errors in these passages. Underline words that are used incorrectly and spell the words correctly on the lines provided. You may use a dictionary to double-check the meanings of words.

1. Andy past the football hire and farther than his brother could. He was sure he wood make the team.

_____ _____ _____

2. Josephine rights about how to keep the piece, not brake it. She wears a flour in her hair.

_____ _____ _____ _____

3. The trapped fox choose threw the rope and freeze itself.

_____ _____ _____

Challenge

4. Other students' phrase may interfere with my writes at school. I chews peace.

_____ _____ _____

Name _____ Date _____

Identifying and Using Personal Pronouns

Focus

A **pronoun** is a word that takes the place of a noun in a sentence. Pronouns that name specific persons or things are called **personal pronouns**. A personal pronoun can replace

Rule	Example
• a singular or plural subject noun.	• The **dog** barked. **It** barked.
• a singular or plural object noun.	• The dog barked at **Iris.** The dog barked at **her.**
• a singular or plural possessive noun.	• Here is **Terrell's** book. Here is **his** book.
• The pronoun I always takes the place of a subject noun. The pronoun me always takes the place of an object noun.	• **I** talked with Trevor. Trevor talked with **me.**

Practice A

Read this paragraph. The pronouns are missing. Write the correct pronoun in each blank so that the paragraph makes sense.

Joshua and Kaitlyn were sure that the hot-air balloon was moving

faster than _____ thought it should be. Kaitlyn looked at Joshua

and told _____ that _____ wasn't scared. Joshua said that

_____ wasn't scared either. Although neither one of _____ was

scared, _____ both agreed to keep talking to each other. Finally,

the pilot of the balloon said, "It's time for _____ to land."

Identifying and Using Personal Pronouns

Practice B Underline the correct pronoun in parentheses for each sentence.

1. (Her, Mine) papers are on the table.

2. The jacket belongs to (I, me).

3. Blue is (my, me) favorite color.

4. (He, His) is wearing a new tie.

5. (Their, They) shoes are wet.

Apply Read this paragraph. If an underlined pronoun is incorrect, write the correct pronoun above it.

The strange men left their enormous wooden boats and waded toward shore. This was the first time that us had seen these people, and us weren't sure what them wanted. We asked one another, "Who are these men? Why are them here? What are those things in theirs hands?" We shall soon see what it want, me thought.

Name _____ **Date** _____

Synonyms

Focus **Synonyms** are words that are similar in meaning.

Practice Complete each set of synonyms with a word from the word box.

hard	actor	healthy	belief
love	story	clue	

1. wholesome; well _____

2. hint; tip _____

3. fable; tale _____

4. like; adore _____

5. trust; faith _____

6. tough; firm _____

7. performer; entertainer _____

Apply   Write a synonym for each word.

8. happy _____

9. path _____

10. large _____

11. possibly _____

12. book _____

13. friend _____

14. burnt _____

15. journal _____

Write a sentence using a synonym for the bold-faced words.

16. **laugh** _____

_____

17. **cry** _____

_____

18. **run** _____

_____

Name _____ **Date** _____

Selection Vocabulary

Focus

colonies (ko' • lə • nēz) *n.* plural of **colony:** a settlement formed by people who have come to a new land (page 271)

skill (skil) *n.* ability to do something (page 272)

astronomy (ə • stro' • nə • mē) *n.* the science of studying the universe outside Earth's atmosphere (page 272)

positions (pə • zi' • shənz) *n.* plural of **position:** a place where things are located (page 272)

site (sīt) *n.* location; place to build (page 275)

capital (ka' • pə • təl) *adj.* where the government is located (page 275)

Practice Circle the word in parentheses that best fits each sentence.

1. We're learning a new (site/skill) at soccer practice tonight.

2. The thirteen original (colonies/positions) had many things in common.

3. My dad bought me a telescope because he knows how much I love (capital/astronomy).

4. The old parking lot would be the perfect (site/skill) for our skateboard park.

5. Have you visited your state's (astronomy/capital) city?

6. Do the (colonies/positions) of the constellations change over time, or stay the same?

Apply Match each word on the left to its definition on the right.

7. colonies

    a. expertise gained through practice

8. astronomy

    b. a place where something can be constructed

9. site

    c. learning about outer space

10. skill

    d. spots where things can be found

11. positions

    e. a group of immigrants living in a new land

12. capital

    f. where the people in government meet

Drawing Conclusions

Focus

Writers provide information in a story to help readers draw conclusions about characters and story events.

Drawing conclusions means taking small pieces of information about a character or story event and using them to make a statement about that character or event.

The **conclusion** may not be stated in the text but should be supported by details in the text.

Practice A

Look through "Benjamin Banneker, Pioneering Scientist." Choose a character or story event and draw a conclusion about it. Write the character's name or the story event. Then, write your conclusion, two sentences from the story with details that support your conclusion, and the page numbers where the sentences are found.

Character or story event: _____

Page: _____ Sentence with details: _____

_____

Page: _____ Sentence with details: _____

_____

_____

Conclusion: _____

Practice B

Read the paragraph and then draw a conclusion. Write the sentences from the paragraph that have details which support your conclusion.

The thin young woman stood as still as the flag that hung motionless in the summer air. Her head was bowed. The audience too was quiet. Suddenly she raised her head and paused, then ran at top speed. She leaped high into the air, clearing the high-jump bar. She jumped from the platform where she had landed, smiled widely, and raised her hands high above her head. The audience cheered and clapped wildly.

Conclusion: _____

_____

Detail: _____

_____

Detail: _____

_____

Apply

Write two sentences with details about a friend or member of your family. Then draw a conclusion about him or her from the details in the sentences. Write the conclusion in the space below.

Sentence: _____

_____

Sentence: _____

_____

Conclusion: _____

Name _____ Date _____

Using Magazines and Other Printed Resources

Find magazines, newspapers, or other printed resources (such as a newsletter) that have information about the topic you chose for your investigation. Choose three different resources that are about the same topic, such as doctors' opinions about herbal medicine. Write the title of the resource, the title of the article, and the date of the publication. Then, write a brief summary of each article.

1. Resource title: _____

Title of article: _____ Date: _____

Summary: _____

_____

_____

2. Resource title: _____

Title of article: _____ Date: _____

Summary: _____

_____

_____

3. Resource title: _____

Title of article: _____ Date: _____

Summary: _____

_____

_____

Write two paragraphs based on the summaries you wrote.
Make sure your paragraphs cover the main topic of the
articles you selected. Remember to answer the questions
who, what, where, when, and *why* as you write about the
topic. Write an interesting title for your paragraphs.

Title: _____

_____

_____

_____

_____

_____

_____

_____

_____

_____

_____

_____

_____

_____

_____

_____

Name _____ **Date** _____

Spelling

Focus Homonyms and homophones are words that sound alike.

- **Homonyms** are words that are spelled the same and sound the same but have different meanings.

- **Homophones** are words that sound the same but have different spellings and meanings.

- Many words have more than one meaning. Understanding the different meanings of words helps you use them correctly.

Practice Find the seven spelling words that have two syllables. Write them wherever they belong under each part of speech heading. You may need to write the words in more than one column.

Nouns	Verbs	Adjectives
1. _____	_____	_____
2. _____	_____	_____
3. _____	_____	_____
4. _____	_____	_____
5. _____	_____	_____
6. _____	_____	_____
7. _____	_____	_____

Word List

1. pitcher
2. spring
3. treat
4. swallow
5. bark
6. train
7. hamper
8. change
9. uniform
10. beat
11. vault
12. yard
13. light
14. stalk
15. splinter
16. second
17. stick
18. current
19. taxes
20. plain

Challenge Words

21. concentrate
22. principal
23. reservation

Apply Read each sentence and think about the meaning of the underlined word. On the next line, write another sentence using a different meaning of the spelling word. You may use a dictionary to look up different meanings of each word.

1. It was difficult to swallow a big bite of peanut butter.

_____

2. Please change into some clean clothes.

_____

3. The soldier wore his dress uniform.

_____

4. He will compete in the pole vault.

_____

5. I liked the second song better.

_____

Challenge

6. Who is the principal French horn player?

_____

7. We drove through the Hopi reservation in New Mexico.

_____

Name _____ **Date** _____

Relative Pronouns

Focus

A **relative pronoun** introduces a part of a sentence, or clause, that describes a noun. A **relative pronoun** *relates* to another noun that comes before it in a sentence. There are five main **relative pronouns:** *that, which, who, whom,* and *whose.*

Example: Benjamin Banneker wrote an almanac **that** contained important information.

Practice   Circle the correct relative pronoun in parentheses.

1. *Tara, Tara* is the television show (that/who) won all those awards.

2. Ingrid James is the actress (who/whom) stars on the show.

3. Paul Wright is the character (whom/whose) I said was my favorite.

4. Jade Cleese is the actress (whom/whose) autograph I got today.

5. Do you still have the magazine (that/which) you read about the actors?

Apply   Write a sentence containing a relative pronoun.

_____

_____

Demonstrative Pronouns

Focus   A **demonstrative pronoun** points out a particular person, place, or thing. *This* and *these* refer to people, places, or things that are nearby. *That* and *those* usually refer to people, places, or things that are farther away.

Example: **This** is a workbook page about grammar. **These** are the books. **That** was the best lunch ever! **Those** were delicious sandwiches.

Practice   Read the paragraph. Circle the correct demonstrative pronoun in each set of parentheses.

Today, I ate two muffins. (These, Those) were the muffins on the table in the middle of the kitchen. (This, That) was the first time I had ever eaten a cranberry or pecan muffin. Because I had never eaten any like (these, those), I wasn't sure I would like them. I was glad I didn't have to worry about (this, that), because the muffins tasted great!

Apply   Write a sentence about a dog you saw at the park. Use a demonstrative pronoun in your sentence.

_____

_____

Write a sentence about some dishes sitting on the counter. Use a demonstrative pronoun in your sentence.

_____

_____

Name _____ Date _____

Latin Roots

Focus Many of the English words we use every day contain parts, or roots, that have been borrowed from much older languages. For example, English words often have roots from the ancient languages of Greek and Latin. These roots may be found in a variety of words, and have the same meaning no matter where you find them. When you know the meaning of a **Latin root,** you can begin to figure out the meaning of the English word that contains it. Here are some common **Latin roots** and their meanings:

trans = "across"   *cred* = "believe"   *aud* = "hear"

hosp = "host"   *anim* = "life"   *cap* = "head"

dent = "tooth"   *doc* = "teach"

The word *dentist* has the Latin root *dent,* which means "tooth." You can tell from the meaning of the Latin root that a dentist is a person who takes care of your teeth. The word *captain* contains the Latin root *cap,* which means "head." You can tell from the meaning of the Latin root that a captain is someone who is the head, or leader, of something, such as a ship.

Practice Read the following Latin roots and their meanings. Write another word containing each Latin root beside the one provided.

1. *act:* "do"; actor _____

2. *struct:* "build"; structure _____

3. *mot:* "move"; motion _____

4. *mem:* "mindful of"; memory _____

5. *volv:* "roll"; evolve _____

Apply The following groups of words all have the same Latin roots. Circle the root that each word has in common. Then examine each word carefully and think of its meaning. Think about what the meanings have in common. Then, choose a definition for the root from the box below and write it in the blank.

sea	alone	to see	empty	move

6. vision, visible, invisible, visual

   The Latin root is **vis.** What does **vis** mean? _____

7. solo, solitary, solitude

   The Latin root is **sol.** What does **sol** mean? _____

8. marine, marina, submarine

   The Latin root is **mar.** What does **mar** mean? _____

9. mobility, mobile, automobile

   The Latin root is **mob.** What does **mob** mean? _____

10. vacant, vacancy, vacuum

    The Latin root is **vac.** What does **vac** mean? _____

Name _____ Date _____

Selection Vocabulary

Focus

rumors (rōō' • mûrz) *n.* plural of **rumor:** a story without proof that passes from person to person (page 286)

distract (di • strakt') *v.* to draw attention away from what someone is doing (page 287)

deserted (di • zûr' • təd) *v.* past tense of **desert:** to leave; to abandon (page 288)

impressed (im • prest') *v.* past tense of **impress:** to make a strong effect on someone's feelings (page 289)

abundance (ə • bun' • dunts) *n.* a large amount (page 289)

elegant (e' • li • gənt) *adj.* rich and fine in quality (page 291)

typical (ti' • pi • kəl) *adj.* average; normal for its kind (page 292)

Practice Write the vocabulary word next to the group of words that have a similar meaning.

1. tasteful; refined; cultivated _____

2. common; familiar; customary _____

3. ampleness; plenty; much _____

4. awed; affected; influenced _____

5. hearsay; gossip; tales _____

6. resigned; ran away; surrendered _____

7. disturb; divert; confuse _____

Apply   Write the word that best fits each clue below.

8. Her dress was long, formal, and beaded. We might call it what?

_____

9. If you have more than enough money, what do you have?

_____

10. What do we call stories that someone spreads about

someone else? _____

11. Keith's mouth dropped open as he watched the magician.

What was Keith? _____

12. Magicians sometimes do this to get the audience to look

somewhere else. What is it? _____

13. What would we call a ghost town? _____

14. Most fourth-graders like recess. This isn't unusual. What

would we say it is? _____

Name _____   Date _____

Map Skills

A map contains several elements that help the user find a variety
of information including direction and distance. A map key
explains specific features on a map. The compass rose displays
the four directions: north, south, east, and west. And a map scale
helps us determine distance on the ground.

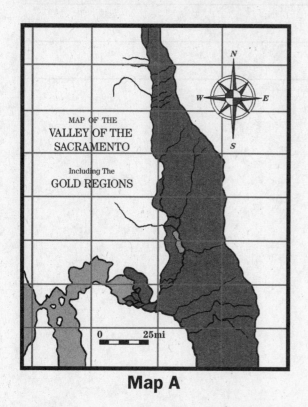

Map A

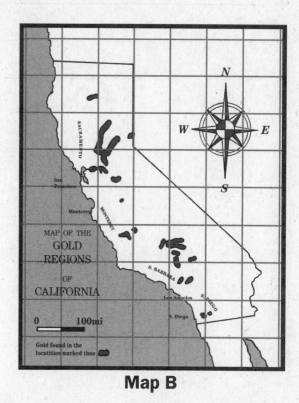

Map B

Identify the map key, the compass rose, and the map scale on these maps.

Write five questions about either Map A or Map B. Give your
questions to a classmate. When your classmate has finished
answering them, discuss the questions. Share how maps could be
useful in your research project for this or other units.

1. _____

2. _____

3. _____

4. _____

5. _____

Name _____ Date _____

Spelling

Focus

- The suffix **-er** means "more."

- **Comparatives** that end in -er are used to compare two things. Sometimes you need to make spelling changes to the base word when you add -er.

- When words end in y, change the y to an i and then add -er.

- In some cases the final consonant doubles when -er is added.

Practice Think about any changes to the base word that were made to make each spelling word a comparative. Write the base word for each spelling word below.

Just add -er:

1. harder _____   2. deeper _____

3. calmer _____   4. louder _____

Change y to i and add -er:

5. cloudier _____   6. earlier _____

Just add r:

7. nicer _____   8. simpler _____

Double the final consonant:

9. dimmer _____   10. wetter _____

Word List
1. harder
2. cloudier
3. thinner
4. happier
5. wetter
6. cuter
7. simpler
8. deeper
9. bolder
10. nicer
11. calmer
12. nearer
13. dimmer
14. louder
15. earlier
16. truer
17. bigger
18. scarier
19. cheaper
20. freer

Challenge Words
21. lonelier
22. quieter

Apply

Look at the phrase in parentheses and read each sentence. Write the spelling word that belongs in each blank.

1. (more true) Robin Hood's aim was _____ than Little John's.

2. (more big) Jumbo was _____ than the other elephants.

3. (more cheap) Large screen televisions are _____ this year.

4. (more near) She scooted _____ to the fire to get warm.

5. (more cute) The cheerleaders think their new outfits are _____.

6. (more scary) I watched a _____ movie on Halloween.

7. (more hard) Mr. Lawrence made up a _____ test.

8. (more bold) The reporter asked a _____ question today.

Challenge:

9. (more quiet) Our class was _____ after lunch.

10. (more lonely) Edward was _____ and sadder than before.

Name _____ Date _____

Superlative Adjectives

Focus

Superlative adjectives compare three or more things. Superlative forms of most one-syllable adjectives end in -*est*.

Example: Raoul is the *tallest* boy in his class.

Add the word *most* to most adjectives with two or more syllables to form their superlatives.

Example: The quiz was the *most challenging* one of the year.

There are always exceptions. For example, *happy* has more than one syllable, but its superlative form is *happiest*.

Practice Write the superlative form of the bold-faced adjectives on the line provided.

1. **loud** _____

2. **quick** _____

3. **generous** _____

4. **pretty** _____

Apply Write a sentence using the superlative form of each adjective.

5. **boring** _____

_____

6. **hard** _____

_____

Irregular Superlative Adjectives

Focus

Some adjectives are **irregular,** or different from other adjectives. Their superlatives are not formed by adding -est or the word most.

Here are some examples:

Adjective	Superlative
good	best
bad	worst
many, much	most
little (amount, not size)	least

Practice

Circle the correct superlative adjective in parentheses.

1. Kya did a good job in the race, but today her sister was (goodest/best).

2. We all have many rocks in our collections, but Shane has the (manyest/most).

3. Fila was upset, because this was her (worst/most bad) performance of the season.

4. Riley has the (most little/least) number of marbles left in her bag.

Apply

Write a sentence using the correct superlative form of each adjective.

5. bad _____

_____

6. many _____

_____

Grammar, Usage, and Mechanics • *Skills Practice 1*

Name _____ Date _____

Greek Roots

Focus

Roots carry meaning. Many words in the English language have **Greek roots**. Knowing what a Greek root means helps you to figure out a word's meaning.

The Greek root **path** means "feeling."

The Greek root **mim** means "to copy or imitate."

The Greek root **nym** means "name."

The Greek root **opt** means "eye."

The Greek root **ortho** means "straight."

Practice

Based on what you know about English words that come from Greek, write a definition for each of the following words or phrases.

1. **sympathy** _____

2. **mimic** _____

3. **optic nerve** _____

_____

4. **orthodontist** _____

5. **synonym** _____

_____

6. **optical illusion** _____

_____

Apply

Based on what you know about English words that come from Greek, match the following words on the left with their definitions on the right.

1. mimeograph

2. optometrist

3. antonym

4. mimicry

5. pathetic

6. mime

7. orthopedics

8. homonyms

a. medical field dealing with straightening bones and joints

b. a duplicating machine

c. causing someone to feel emotion for you

d. one animal imitating another

e. a word that means the opposite of another word

f. an actor who copies someone else using only gestures

g. an eye doctor

h. words that mean the same but are spelled differently

Name _____ Date _____

Selection Vocabulary

Focus

associations (ə • sō' • sē • ā' • shənz) *n.* plural of **association:** a friendship and connection (page 302)

detained (di • tānd') *v.* past tense of **detain:** to keep back (page 302)

vast (vast) *adj.* large; widespread (page 303)

engaged (in • gā' • jd) *adj.* busy with (page 306)

tremendous (tri • men' • dəs) *adj.* very large (page 312)

provisions (prə • vi' • zhənz) *n.* plural of **provision:** a supply of food and other necessary items (page 313)

permanent (pûr' • mə • nənt) *adj.* lasting; not temporary (page 315)

Practice Write the vocabulary word that best matches the underlined word or phrase in the sentences below.

1. Babysitting is a <u>very big</u> responsibility. _____

2. I have kept a lot of <u>friendships and acquaintances</u> from my old neighborhood.

   _____

3. Training her new dog keeps Lindee constantly <u>occupied</u>.

   _____

4. Is this going to be our <u>unchanging</u> seating arrangement?

   _____

5. My grandpa's farmland is <u>widespread</u>. _____

Apply Write the word from the word box that matches each definition below.

6. _____ extremely huge

7. _____ not going to change

8. _____ partners or companions

9. _____ delayed

10. _____ participating in

11. _____ stretching out far and wide

12. _____ things that are needed

Name _____ Date _____

Gathering Information

Before you begin to gather information, decide on a topic to research for your investigation.

• My group's topic:

_____

• Information I need to find or figure out about my topic:

_____

_____

_____

_____

Complete the chart below to help you decide which sources will be useful.

Sources	Useful?	How?
Encyclopedias		
Books		
Magazines		
Newspapers		
Videotapes, filmstrips, etc.		
Television		
Interviews, observations		
Museums		
Other		

Presenting Information

How might you present the information that you found to your classmates? You could make a poster or chart, build a tabletop model, or even create a videotape.

- Write information you found on your topic.

_____

_____

_____

_____

_____

_____

_____

- List some of the ways you might present your information.

_____

_____

_____

_____

_____

_____

_____

Letters to the Editor

Think

Audience: Who will read your letter to the editor?

_____

Purpose: What is your reason for writing a letter to the editor?

_____

_____

Practice

Use the space below to organize the ideas for the body of your letter to the editor.

Write the problem or issue that concerns you: _____

Write your opinion about the problem or issue:

_____

Write the reasons that support your opinion:

_____

_____

_____

Write why your readers should agree with your opinion:

_____

_____

Revising

Use this checklist to revise your letter to the editor.

☐ Did you support your opinion with facts and examples?

☐ Did you use the correct format to organize your letter?

☐ Does your letter show that you have strong feelings about the problem you address?

Editing/Proofreading

Use this checklist to correct mistakes.

☐ Did you check all names and places for correct spelling?

☐ Did you check all punctuation and capitalization?

☐ Did you check the punctuation of the heading, inside address, salutation, and closing?

Publishing

Use this checklist to get ready for publication.

☐ Write or type a neat final copy.

☐ Fold the letter, place it in an envelope, address it to the editor, stamp it, and mail it.

Name _____ **Date** _____

Spelling

Focus

- The suffix **-est** means "most."
- **Superlatives** that end in -est are used to compare many things.
- Sometimes you need to make spelling changes to the base word when you add -est.
- For words that end in e, just add -st.
- For words that end in y, change the y to i before adding -est.
- In some cases the final consonant doubles when -est is added.

Practice Think about any changes that were made to make each spelling word a superlative. Write the base word for each spelling word below.

Just add -est:

1. sharpest _____   2. brightest _____

3. narrowest _____   4. oldest _____

Change y to i and add -est:

5. clumsiest _____   6. fanciest _____

Just add -st:

7. gentlest _____   8. noblest _____

Double the final consonant:

9. gladdest _____   10. hottest _____

Word List

1. hottest
2. neatest
3. fullest
4. oldest
5. bravest
6. sweetest
7. brightest
8. fondest
9. clumsiest
10. dearest
11. sharpest
12. gentlest
13. smoothest
14. gloomiest
15. gladdest
16. narrowest
17. fittest
18. heaviest
19. noblest
20. fanciest

Challenge Words

21. friendliest
22. scarcest

Challenge:

These spelling words have more than one suffix. Write the base word for each one.

11. gloomiest _____   **12.** friendliest _____

Apply Look at the base word in parentheses and read each sentence. Write the correct comparative or superlative form of each spelling word in the blank.

1. (most noble) The fierce warrior had the _____ goal.

2. (more gloomy) Eeyore is _____ than Pooh.

3. (most smooth) His dog has the _____ coat.

4. (most dear) Kate is the _____ young woman.

5. (more brave) The lion felt _____ than before.

6. (most fond) She is _____ of roses.

7. (more full) The moon looks _____ tonight.

8. (more heavy) Gold is _____ than silver.

Challenge:

9. (most scarce) Safe drinking water is _____ in Africa.

10. (more friendly) Marcus is _____ than Logan.

Comparative Adjectives

> **Focus**
>
> A **comparative adjective** compares two things.
>
> **Comparative adjectives** add *-er* to most one-syllable adjectives. Use *more* in front of most adjectives with two or more syllables, but do not add *-er* to the end of the adjective.
>
> Examples: My cat is *bigger* than my sister's cat.
> My sister's cat is *more active* than mine.

Practice Write the comparative form of the bold-faced adjectives on the line provided.

1. **great** _____

2. **quick** _____

3. **creative** _____

4. **pretty** _____

5. **optimistic** _____

6. **hopeful** _____

7. **smart** _____

Apply Write a sentence using the comparative form of each adjective.

8. **interested** _____

_____

9. **old** _____

_____

Irregular Comparative Adjectives

Some adjectives are **irregular,** or different from other adjectives. Their comparatives are not formed by adding -*er* or the word *more*.

Some adjectives such as *good*, *bad*, and *many* have different comparative forms.

Adjective	Comparative
good	better
bad	worse
many, much	more
little (amount, not size)	less

Practice Circle the correct comparative adjective in parentheses.

1. This route takes (less/least) time.

2. I need (mucher/more) eggs if I'm going to make breakfast for everyone.

3. Hannah has a (worst/worse) headache now than she did this morning.

4. I'll try to get a (better/gooder) score next time.

5. There has to be a (best/better) way to organize those supplies.

6. Where can I get (more/most) sand for the sandbox?

Apply Write a sentence using the correct comparative form of each adjective.

7. good _____

8. bad _____

Name _____ Date _____

Contractions

Practice A   Write each of the following contractions as two words.

1. shouldn't _____

2. they've _____

3. she's _____

4. what's _____

5. can't _____

6. we'd _____

7. wasn't _____

8. he'll _____

Some contractions are formed from a pronoun and the helping verb *will* or the helping or main verb *have*. When you make these words into contractions, the *wi* and the *ha* are replaced with apostrophes.

Practice B

Rewrite the following sentences, changing the underlined words to a contraction.

9. <u>I will</u> buy your ticket for you.

_____

10. I think <u>they have</u> already eaten.

_____

11. <u>You will</u> never guess what just happened.

_____

12. <u>We have</u> got four home games left.

_____

13. <u>They will</u> be back later.

_____

Apply

The following contractions have been formed incorrectly. Write the correct spelling of each contraction on the lines provided.

14. willn't _____

15. she'ill _____

16. cann't _____

17. havn't _____

18. shalln't _____

Name _____ Date _____

Selection Vocabulary

Focus

politics (po' • lə • tiks) *pl. n.* the activity of government *and* running for offices (page 329)

legislator (le' • jəs • lā' • tor') *n.* a member of the part of government that makes laws (page 329)

debates (di • bāts') *n.* plural of **debate:** a public discussion of issues by people who disagree (page 331)

intelligence (in • te' • lə • jənts) *n.* the ability to think, learn, and understand (page 332)

rebelling (ri • bel'• ing) *v.* form of **rebel:** to fight against authority (page 334)

liberty (li' • bûr • tē) *n.* the freedom to act, think, or speak as one pleases (page 335)

Practice Write the vocabulary word next to the group of words that have a similar meaning.

1. emancipation; freedom; liberation _____

2. understanding; ability; aptitude _____

3. arguments; disagreements; fights _____

4. affairs; activities; government _____

5. lawmaker; law-passer; law-giver _____

6. disobeying; revolting; uprising _____

Apply Circle the word in parentheses that best fits each sentence.

7. Jude wants to be a (legislator/liberty) so he can make new laws.

8. Forbes wasn't (debates/rebelling) against his parents; he just asked them why he couldn't go.

9. These quizzes are designed to test your (politics/intelligence).

10. My parents enjoy being involved in local (liberty/politics).

11. Not every country enjoys the (legislator/liberty) we do.

12. The candidates held a series of (intelligence/debates) to argue over some important issues.

Name _____ Date _____

Historical Fiction

Think

Audience: Who will read your historical fiction?

_____

Purpose: What is your reason for writing historical fiction?

_____

_____

_____

Prewriting

Use this graphic organizer to plan your historical fiction.

In historical fiction, the	In my story, the
setting is a certain time and place in the past.	setting:
characters act how people of that time would have acted.	characters:
plot includes events or problems from that time.	plot:
details such as clothing, home, and transportation are true to the setting.	details:

Revising
Use this checklist to revise your historical fiction.

☐ Do your words clearly describe the time and place?

☐ Does your plot deal with problems or events from that time and place?

☐ Does the story sound like it could have really happened?

Editing/Proofreading
Use this checklist to correct mistakes.

☐ Did you check all names and places for correct spelling?

☐ Did you check all punctuation and capitalization?

Publishing
Use this checklist to get ready for publication.

☐ Check your story for any final errors.

☐ Write or type a neat final copy.

Name _____ **Date** _____

Spelling

Focus

- A **contraction** is a shortened form of two or more words.
- When the words are joined together, an apostrophe is used to take the place of at least one letter or word.
- Some contractions look the same, but have different possible meanings.

Practice A

Write the spelling contractions under the words they stand for. The first one is done for you.

had, would

1. they'd

2. _____

is, has

4. _____   6. _____

5. _____

not

7. _____   11. _____

8. _____   12. _____

9. _____   13. _____

10. _____

3. _____

Challenge:

14. _____

Word List

1. I'm
2. don't
3. he'll
4. weren't
5. it's
6. can't
7. hasn't
8. we'll
9. we're
10. she's
11. we'd
12. o'clock
13. you'd
14. they'd
15. I'll
16. won't
17. isn't
18. wasn't
19. that's
20. we've

Challenge Words

21. would've
22. doesn't

Practice B **Write the contraction for each phrase.**

15. I am _____

16. were not _____

17. he will _____

18. you would _____

19. that is _____

20. do not _____

21. we have _____

22. we are _____

23. is not _____

Challenge

24. would have _____   25. does not _____

Underline five errors in the paragraph. Write the words correctly on the lines provided.

At five o'clock well leave for the show. Craig willn't be able to join us, so aisle drive. Wern't you going to buy extra tickets? Carson said heed like to come along.

26. _____

27. _____

28. _____

29. _____

30. _____